*Uniforms of
the Elite Forces*

Leroy Thompson

Uniforms of the Elite Forces

Illustrated by
Michael Chappell

BLANDFORD PRESS
Poole   Dorset

First published in the U.K. 1982 by Blandford Press,
Link House, West Street, Poole, Dorset BH15 1LL

Distributed in the United States by
Sterling Publishing Co., Inc.,
2 Park Avenue, New York, N.Y. 10016

ISBN 0 7137 1259 7

Photoset in Monophoto Apollo
by Asco Trade Typesetting Ltd., Hong Kong
and Printed by South China Printing Co., Hong Kong

Contents

A Short History of Elite Forces

The elite military unit is by no means a modern creation. In fact, as long as there has been warfare, certain fighting men have been formed into groups and assigned the most difficult or dangerous missions. In ancient history, the elite force usually took the form of a shock unit committed to turn the tide of battle at some critical moment. Alexander's Companions, the Theban Sacred Band, and the Persian Immortals were such elites. Often these elite troops served the secondary purpose of acting as bodyguards to the soldier king, but under the Romans and the Byzantines, the bodyguard function became an end unto itself, and eventually the Praetorians even became king (or to be more precise, emperor) makers. This was also true to some extent of the Varangians in Byzantium.

In the Middle Ages there was a dichotomy among elite forces. Because of birth and the military system of the time, mounted knights were considered the military elite of feudal armies, while based on performance, at least in the late Middle Ages, specialists like the English longbowman and the Swiss pikeman were the true elites. Each in his own way could defeat the mounted knight, the bowman by keeping him at a distance with missiles and the pikeman by standing fast in the face of a charge. The longbowmen and the pikemen were elites created by the weapons they used and their skill with them.

Another elite from this time period were the Byzantine cataphracts, skilled professional heavy cavalry who could also use the bow. Because of their much deserved reputation as one of the toughest armies in history, the Mongols could also be called a military elite.

By the Renaissance the elites in many armies were the arquebusiers or musketeers who could wield the new gunpowder weapons, but perhaps the most famous elite of the time were the Janissaries of the Ottoman Empire. Raised from childhood as soldiers, the Janissaries helped create and hold together the vast Ottoman Empire for hundreds of years.

As technology began to dominate the battlefield in the nineteenth century elite forces were still used to turn the tide of battle. Napoleon's Old Guard or the Union Iron Brigade (interestingly enough the forerunner of the 101st Airborne Division) were typical examples of elite shock troops. It was the Prussian Army, however, which created a unique type of elite soldier during the latter nineteenth century. Historically, the elite soldier has been highly skilled as a fighting man, but the Prussian elite were the members of the General Staff – desk soldiers, planners who fought their battles over maps. Another odd elite of the nineteenth century was the Light Brigade which became an elite unit in the public mind after the fact, not because of a victory but because like many future elites they were forced by incompetent generalship to fight courageously but unsupported against artillery.

During World War I, the immobility of trench warfare limited the scope for elite units. Still, there were troops who have to be considered elite. The airmen, for example, who pioneered warfare in a new medium were the romantic elite. Because of the high quality of the initial BEF contingent, the 'Old Contemptibles' were, in fact, an elite group as well. So were the U.S. Marines. As usual ahead of his time, Billy Mitchell even wanted to convert the U.S. 1st Infantry Division to an airborne division by 1919. But, it was the Germans who really created an elite unit akin to today's elite forces. These were the German Stormtroopers who appeared in 1918. Trained to infiltrate behind Allied lines and disrupt communications and supply, the Stormtroopers were forerunners of the elite raiders of World War II and today.

In the years between World Wars I and II, the use of the parachute gave birth to a new elite soldier – the paratrooper. The Soviets were the first to realize the potential of airborne troops,

2

and by 1935 were capable of massed drops of over 5,000 military parachutists. These troops were trained to take advantage of their airmobility, too, being skilled saboteurs who could operate behind enemy lines.

The Italians were close behind the Soviets in military parachuting and had parachute units trained and operational by the late 1930s. The Italians were also pioneers in another type of elite unit having used military frogmen as early as World War I and continuing to train underwater raiders and saboteurs in large quantity in the years leading up to World War II.

The Germans who had been training in the Soviet Union to circumvent restrictions on their armed forces were quite impressed with Soviet demonstrations of the use of airborne and gliderborne troops. As a result, the Germans also in the 1930s began training military parachutists.

France, Great Britain, Japan, and the United States lagged behind the USSR, Italy, and Germany, but by 1941, all were training military parachutists. In the case of the United States and Britain, however, it was not until the successes of German parachute and glider troops in the assault on the Low Countries in 1940 that the training of parachute troops really got under way.

Although the German drops at Rotterdam and the Hague are sometimes credited with being the first combat use of paratroopers, this is incorrect. The Germans themselves had dropped airborne troops earlier in the invasion of Denmark and Norway, and the Soviets had used paratroopers in small unit drops against bandits as early as 1936. Soviet airborne troops had also jumped (sometimes without parachutes into snow drifts) in the Winter War against Finland. It was the German *Fallschirmjäger*, however, who made the first major successful airborne assaults and convinced the more conventional military hierarchies of the potential value of parachute and glider troops. The fact that both Winston Churchill and Franklin Roosevelt were greatly impressed with the idea of airborne troops also lent impetus to the development of airborne armies in the U.S. and Great Britain.

During World War II, hundreds of thousands of parachute

3

troops were trained, though many of them never made a combat jump. This was especially true in the Soviet Union where airborne troops were trained and then converted to guards infantry divisions to be fed into the meatgrinders at Moscow and Stalingrad. These former airborne troops contributed significantly in halting the German advance, acting as shock troops or helping to stiffen units composed of conscripts.

The Soviets did launch two major airborne assaults, at Vyazma and at the Dnieper Loop, but neither was particularly successful. Soviet airborne forces performed most effectively in small unit drops where they carried out daring raids. An operation of this type at Demyansk was the forerunner of what the Soviets today call 'desant' missions. Though shrouded in secrecy, there were also NKVD raiding and sabotage units who jumped and operated behind enemy lines.

Despite their early successes, the German paratroopers spent much of the war serving as elite infantry, seeing especially tough fighting in Russia and in Italy. After the early airborne victories in Holland and Belgium, Hitler grew overconfident in the ability of unsupported parachute troops, and the *Fallschirmjäger* was in 1941 decimated in the attack on Crete. After that, parachute troops were rarely used by the Germans for airborne operations, though a few small unit drops, including one behind allied lines during the Ardennes offensive, were attempted. A small number of paratroopers were assigned to Otto Skorzeny, also, and they were trained as what today would be called para-commandos.

Compared to the other belligerents, the Japanese did not train a large number of parachute troops. At the beginning of the war, a naval reinforced battalion, the Yokosuka Special Naval Landing Force, and an army airborne brigade were available for parachute operations. Like most pre-war Japanese special units, both airborne forces were highly trained and motivated. In the first weeks of the war, both were used in classic airborne assaults when they dropped to seize key airfields and oil refineries. Not until late 1944 when a parachute assault was launched against American airfields in the Philippines were Japanese paratroopers

4

dropped in any number again, though.

The United States and Great Britain made up for their late start by training large numbers of airborne troops during the war. Eventually, the U.S. had five airborne divisions plus some independent parachute infantry regiments, and the British had two divisions as well as some independent formations. Both countries foresaw the use of large airborne armies in mass drops as the best employment of airborne troops, and the drops in Normandy, Holland, and across the Rhine were most typical of British and American airborne operations.

Early in the war, the British did make use of airborne troops for raids at Monte Volturno in Southern Italy and Bruneval on the French coast, but, in general, raiding missions were left to other troops. The U.S. also concentrated primarily on large operations but employed airborne raiders on occasion as in the rescue of POWs from Los Banos Prison Camp in the Philippines in which U.S. Rangers, U.S. paratroopers, and local guerrillas worked together. Since they were not mass drops, many of the most fascinating U.S. airborne operations took place in the Pacific theater, the jump by the 503rd Parachute Infantry Regiment on Corregidor being one of the most difficult airborne assaults of the war.

Although the development and use of airborne troops during World War II is a milestone which has had a decisive influence on elite units from then on, another occurrence must be considered of equal importance in the history of modern elite forces, and that was the formation in 1940 of the British Commandos. Although some Commandos were also parachute trained, they were primarily amphibious raiders, and their successes stimulated the formation of all types of other raiding units. Two pieces of Commando equipment were also destined to become standards for future elite units. Because silent killing was an important skill for hit and run raiders, the Commandos were given extensive training in hand-to-hand combat and the use of the knife. Their instructors, Capts Fairbairn and Sykes, designed an efficient and distinctive fighting knife for the Commandos, and to this day the dagger, in many cases closely patterned on the F-S stiletto, is an important piece of symbolic and practical equipment for elite units. Although other units such as the German panzer forces had previously worn berets, it was the Commandos who truly established the beret as the symbol of an elite fighting force. Even more than the distinctive blade, the beret has now been adopted by virtually all elite forces.

Within the British Army, the Commandos engendered all sorts of offspring. Most famous, of course, is the Special Air Service. Founded in 1941 in the Western Desert by David Stirling, the SAS was a parachute qualified unit trained for raiding missions deep in Axis controlled territory. The SAS was also effectively employed behind German lines in France and Italy where raiding parties operating out of French forests and in the mountains of northern Italy aided the Resistance and harassed German supply lines in support of the Allied advance out of Normandy.

Often confused with the SAS was the Long Range Desert Group. (The SAS was closely associated, however, with the LRDG in the Western Desert.) The LRDG were not really raiders but were scouts. Like today's LRRPs, they were trained to penetrate enemy lines and to scout enemy positions without being detected.

Another Commando offspring was the Combined Operations Assault Pilotage Parties whose job was to survey enemy beaches for possible landing sites and to destroy obstacles in preparation for amphibious landings. The COPPs used small canoes to slip ashore or swam into the beaches. They were cousins of the U.S. frogmen and predecessors of today's para-frogmen or combat swimmers. The Sea Reconnaissance Unit (SRU) was a similar group of British combat swimmers who made more extensive use of breathing apparatus, and another related group was the Special Boat Service, orginally forming part of the SAS, which made raids using two man canoes and small craft such as Kayaks. The Royal Marines also had their canoe raiders.

The U.S. Navy also trained and made extensive use of frogmen, but it was the Army's Rangers and Marine Raiders which were the true U.S. offshoots of the Commandos. Unless drawn from parachute units, the World War II Rangers were not jump qualified but were highly trained along Commando lines as amphibious raiders or spearheaders for amphibious landings. The U.S. Marine Raiders were a controversial group, since it was felt with much justification that all U.S. Marines were skilled amphibious raiders and a special unit was not necessary. Still, the Raiders along with the Marine parachute troops, the Para-Marines, proved to be an elite within an elite and were held in awe even by the tough fleet Marines.

Perhaps the most underrated U.S. special unit of World War II was the First Special Service Force. Actually, it is incorrect to call the Force a U.S. unit since it was composed of U.S. and Canadian personnel. Originally chosen for raids in Norway using a tracked snow vehicle, Force members were trained as paratroopers, ski troops, mountain troops, and amphibious Commandos. Many qualified observers feel the 1st S.S.F. may have been the toughest combat unit of World War II.

The Italians did not realize the early promise of their airborne program but did score many successes with their frogmen during the war, including the planting of mines on British ships at Gibraltar. The Germans had frogmen as well and a special unit, the Brandenburgers, earmarked for commando missions. Many Brandenburgers were later incorporated into Otto Skorzeny's *Jagdverbande*.

The Free French formed their own SAS units as well as parachute and commando forces. In most cases, the French formations operated under British auspices. Dutch and Belgian parachute units were also formed from troops who had fled to England when the Germans occupied their countries.

By the end of World War II, this wide assortment of special units had proven their value in combat. Special forces had shown that they could undertake difficult, even seemingly impossible, missions behind enemy lines and could tie down large numbers of enemy troops on garrison duty to defend against small unit raids. There were many critics of the elite forces, though. They felt that many of the men who should have been NCOs or junior officers in conventional units were serving as privates in elite units, causing a loss of good junior leadership in the armies as a whole. This was part of what has been called the 'selection-destruction cycle' of elite units. According to this theory, elite forces siphon off the best men who then suffer much higher casualties than normal because of their high motivation and the dangerous missions they are sent on. To counter these arguments, it should be pointed out that often men who excel in elite forces get bored or disillusioned with the peacetime paper shuffling and drill in conventional units and leave the armed forces; whereas, in elite units they render valuable service to their country.

There is no doubt that the elite units suffered very high casualties in World War II, but this was due in many cases to their improper employment. Higher ranking officers failing to realize that elite forces were too lightly armed to engage in pitched battles with conventional enemy units having artillery and tank support foolishly committed the paratroopers or rangers in situations where they were forced to substitute courage for heavy weapons, and they were decimated as a result.

As soon as the war ended, the United States and Great Britain began to cut back their military manpower drastically. Three out of the five U.S. airborne divisions were de-activated shortly after the cessation of hostilities, while some British parachute units as well as the SAS were reduced or disbanded. The Commandos were all consolidated under the Royal Marines and cut to one brigade with a strength of 2,200 men.

The Soviets, however, continued to expand their airborne forces as they did all aspects of their armed forces. But, they put special emphasis on the airborne forces, realizing they were excellent tools for rapidly deploying Soviet might to herd satellite countries back into the fold if they strayed from Moscow's line.

Many other countries, large and small, added airborne troops and/or commandos to their armed forces in the immediate post-war years. The French were particularly energetic in raising parachute units to serve in their African and Indo-Chinese colonies. By 1950, both colonial and Foreign Legion parachute battalions were in service alongside metropolitan parachute formations. France also kept an SAS unit for service in Indo-China.

Throughout the period between 1947 and 1954, the French paras had plenty of chances to make combat jumps. During that seven year time span, the French made more than 100 combat jumps in Indo-China, a large number of them in battalion strength or greater. All of this activity, plus the fact that the paras and Foreign Legionnaires (especially the famous 1st and 2nd BEP) were the only troops which could be relied on for aggressive action in Indo-China, granted the French paras an elite position in the French armed forces even above that normally held by airborne troops. The paras, in fact, soon began to view themselves as answerable only to para officers and to no one else. This attitude would eventually contribute to the revolt of some parachute units in Algeria in later years.

In the early days of the Korean War, the United States found itself unprepared, and from the poor performance of some of the American conscript units early in the war, it was obvious some stiffening was needed. The arrival of the U.S. Marines helped, as did the transfer of the 187th Airborne Regimental Combat Team to Korea. Although the U.S. Airborne Rangers and the U.N. Partisan Force made some combat jumps, the major U.N. Combat drops in Korea were all carried out by the 187th.

Royal Marine Commandos once again proved their value in Korea by raiding North Korean installations along the coast and tying a large number of Communist troops down garrisoning their seaboard. Commandos and the SAS also in the 1950s performed yeoman service in Malaya, the SAS proving especially skilled in counterinsurgency operations. The fighting in Malaya foreshadowed the type of guerrilla warfare that the West would be fighting for the next 25 years, and the SAS's success emphasized the need for highly trained elite units to deal with Communist insurgents. Korea and Indo-China also brought home the fact that airborne troops were still a highly viable weapon, but it did seem as if the day of the divisional sized airborne assault was past. The regimental, brigade, battalion, or company sized airborne operation would be the more likely use of parachute troops in the future.

During the early to mid-1950's, the Israelis felt the need for a special type of elite unit to stage retaliation raids against Palestinians in Jordan. The initial unit, designated '101', consisted of only forty-five men who carried out many successful strikes. Eventually, however, '101' merged with the paratroopers and a new raiding unit, '202', was born. Units 101 and 202 were the forerunners of the Israeli paratroopers and commandos who have established a worldwide reputation for their ability to undertake and succeed at seemingly impossible missions.

After the fall of Dien Bien Phu, many French paras went into captivity, but French airborne operations continued in Algeria after the withdrawal from Indo-China where Foreign Legion paras were the primary striking units against the rebels.

A landmark airborne operation took place in November 1956, at Suez when British and French paratroopers made a combat jump, while Royal Marine Commandos staged an amphibious and helicopter assault in conjunction with the parachute operation. This was the first major combined parachute, airmobile, and amphibious assault in history. Even before the British/French paratroopers went out of the door over Suez, Israeli paratroopers and commandos had been in action against the Egyptians at Tor and the Mitla Pass.

Throughout the 1950s and early 1960s, a pattern emerged among western countries for the use of elite units. In colonies or former colonies, the elite forces were used to fight terrorists or insurgents. The SAS, Parachute Regiment, and Royal Marine Commandos were in Malaya, Borneo, Aden, and Oman fighting terrorists or guerrillas. French paras fought in Indo-China and North Africa. Spanish paratroopers made combat jumps in the Sahara, and Portuguese and Belgian paratroopers were in action in Africa. The United States also used its elite troops for intervention in Lebanon where the Marines were landed and in the Dominican Republic where the 82nd Airborne was committed. The role of elite troops as 'trouble shooters' was being established.

10

This role made sense for elite forces, too. Paratroopers or commandos are trained to travel light, operate in small groups, penetrate into enemy territory, and survive and fight under difficult conditions. All of these skills are particularly suited to counter-insurgency warfare. Equally important, the elite troops are volunteers and professionals. As a result, there is much less pressure on elected governments if a few 'pros' get killed in a jungle or desert somewhere than if the same thing happens to conscripts. And being professionals, a much lower percentage of the elite troops will suffer casualties fighting guerrillas.

In 1952, the United States organized the Special Forces as specialists in guerrilla warfare. Airborne qualified, trained in foreign weapons and guerrilla methods, and expert linguists, the Special Forces were intended to operate behind enemy lines raising and training pro-U.S. partisans or guerrillas. Ironically, based on a 'set a thief to catch a thief' philosophy and like most other elite troops in the West, the Special Forces have been utilized throughout most of their history on counterguerrilla operations. During the 1950s and up until the death of President Kennedy, who was a great patron of the 'Green Berets', the Special Forces were, however, involved in true guerrilla operations in South America and the Caribbean, including missions in Cuba. It still is not clear what part the Special Forces played in some Central and South American revolutions, but play a part they did.

Special units within the U.S. Navy and U.S. Marine Corps were also occasionally called upon for special missions during the 1950s and early 60s. The Marines' Force Recon troops not only completed the tough Marine basic and AIT (Advanced Infantry Training) but were also jump qualified and trained as combat swimmers. The Navy's UDT (Underwater Demolition Teams) or frogmen have been the primary underwater elite of the U.S. armed forces since World War II, but the Marine Recons, U.S. Special Forces, U.S.A.F. Pararescue, and the Navy's own SEALs (Sea, Air, Land) have also been involved in underwater training and operations. The SEALs, formed in 1962, are trained as paratroopers, frogmen, and elite light infantry. In addition to this already rather comprehensive training, many SEALs are currently put through the training program of an elite unit of one of the U.S.'s allies to develop additional skills. All of these U.S. elite units plus hundreds of thousands of conventional troops got their chance to prove themselves in Vietnam, especially the elite units.

As early as 1957, U.S. Special Forces teams were 'in country' training Vietnamese Rangers, and in 1960 more than 100 'Green Berets' led by the most famous 'Beret' of all, 'Bull' Simons, were in Laos training Muong tribesmen. The real Special Forces buildup started in 1961, though, with the beginnings of the CIDG (Civilian Irregular Defense Group) program in which the Special Forces trained and advised hamlet militias to defend themselves against the Viet Cong. The U.S. Special Forces worked in conjunction with the LLDB (the Vietnamese Special Forces) on this program.

The Special Forces also gave more intensive training to groups of full-time indigenous troops called 'strike forces'. These units undertook offensive sweeps searching for the enemy. In May 1964, the Special Forces became involved in one of the most successful but least well-known programs of the war when MACV/SOG (Military Assistance Command Vietnam/Special Operations Group) started 'Project Delta'. The Delta force was trained for long range recon missions into enemy territory to gather intelligence or commit acts of sabotage. Delta teams were composed of U.S. Special Forces, LLDB, and highly trained 'cidgees'. Later SOG projects like 'Sigma' and 'Omega' would evolve from Delta, and eventually SOG units would be operating in Laos, Cambodia, and North Vietnam.

1964 also saw the creation of another elite unit within the CIDG with the beginnings of the Mobile Strike Forces (MIKE Forces) which were airborne trained and acted as a mobile reserve under Special Forces control. MIKE Forces were also used for special recon missions.

When the U.S. committed itself more heavily in Vietnam, the first major combat unit sent to Vietnam was the 173rd Airborne Brigade. Eventually both the 82nd and 101st Airborne Divisions as well as the 1st Air Cav which contained airborne elements would also serve in Vietnam, though the only major combat jump was made by the 173rd Airborne. There were, however, many airborne insertions of Special Forces, SEALs, Marine Recons, LRRPs, and other small elite units, including many from SOG. Both ARVN paratroopers and MIKE Force troops also made parachute assaults.

U.S. combat swimmers, especially the SEALs, were used extensively for raiding in the Mekong Delta, and the SEALs penetrated into Haiphong Harbor and reportedly into Hanoi itself on special missions.

Although large numbers of U.S. ground troops served in Vietnam, it was a war in which elite forces abounded. In addition to those already mentioned, the Army's LRRPs (Long Range Reconnaissance Patrols) and USAF Combat Security Police were trained for special missions, the former to scout in enemy territory and the latter to aggressively defend U.S. airbases by setting small unit ambushes and acting as an elite strike force. Air Force Combat Controllers and Pararescue troops also undertook many dangerous and unheralded operations behind enemy lines. Finally, U.S. Marine ground forces carried the burden of fighting in the I Corps tactical zone.

Throughout the war, Col., later General, Donald Blackburn advocated using the Special Forces to destroy important bridges, dams, factories, etc. inside of North Vietnam, but 'political' considerations legislated against this aggressive use of elite raiders. The Son Tay raid, although not successful in freeing POWs, did show just how vulnerable the North was to such attacks. In fact, a large number of Chinese or Russian advisors were killed at a compound near Son Tay during the raid, and this caused Hanoi a great deal of problems with her Communist allies who felt the North Vietnamese were incapable of even defending their own country. Blackburn, by the way, had made his start in guerrilla warfare in the Philippines during World War II when he led a guerrilla unit known as 'Blackburn's Headhunters'. He later headed MACV/SOG.

In addition to U.S. elite units, the Republic of Vietnam had similar units trained to perform the same types of missions. Also serving in Vietnam were some very tough marines and rangers from the Republic of Korea and SAS troops from Australia and New Zealand. At least some Royal Thai airborne troops fought in Laos as well.

After the U.S. 'disengagement' in Vietnam, many former members of American elite forces went to Rhodesia and joined units like the Rhodesian Light Infantry, Selous Scouts, or Rhodesian SAS where they continued to fight against Communist guerrillas alongside the Rhodesians. All three of these units were eventually composed of parachute trained troops, and many cross border raids were mounted successfully by 'troopies' from these units.

By the 1970s virtually every country in the world, no matter how small, had some type of airborne commando unit available for special missions. In a return to the ancient use of elite forces, many of the para-commandos in developing countries also served as the 'palace guard'.

Although elite units still carry out 'traditional' operations like the 1978 jumps by the French 2nd REP at Kolwezi, the last few years have seen another shift in emphasis among many elite units towards countering urban terrorism. The murder of Israeli athletes at the Munich Olympics in 1972 prompted both the Israelis and the West Germans to develop the capability to deal with terrorist kidnappings and hijackings. The resulting successes of the Israeli '269' Commandos at Entebbe and the German GSG-9 at Mogadishu proved that training elite units for such operations was justified. The British Special Air Service, Dutch Marine Commandos, and Indonesian PMB Counterterrorist unit have all proven their worth in this same type of counterterrorist mission during the last few years.

British elite forces have also served in Ulster in an anti-terrorist role, the SAS, Royal Marine Commandos, and Parachute Regiment all putting in their time. In some cases, the SAS was so successful in its 'covert' operations in Ulster that those who feel terrorists should be handled with kid gloves became upset. Royal

Marine Commando units are now charged with the additional mission of responding to any threat to the North Sea oil fields.

Israeli commandos and paratroopers make cross border raids against Palestinian guerrilla camps almost as a matter of course, and this helps keep Israel's elite units in a high state of readiness.

Reflecting its own concern with the Middle East, the United States has committed a large number of its elite units, including the 82nd Airborne Division and a U.S. Marine Division, to the Rapid Deployment Force. Counterterrorist responsibility within the U.S. armed forces rests with Special Forces Operational Group – Delta, a highly trained unit with a strong commitment to not repeat the fiasco of the attempted Iranian hostage rescue.

The Soviet Union also uses its elite forces as the cutting edge of its foreign policy. Much of the fighting in Afghanistan has been borne by airborne units, and Soviet airborne forces have been used as threats to keep Warsaw Pact allies in line. In the 1968 invasion of Czechoslovakia the airborne forces were more than a threat, spearheading the Soviet move into that country. Special para-commando battalions are earmarked for 'desant' missions to assassinate key NATO leaders, destroy nuclear weapons stockpiles, and otherwise create confusion behind NATO lines should the balloon go up in Western Europe. Another Soviet elite force, the Naval Infantry, has also assumed an important role as Soviet naval power allows them to project the 'black berets' to far parts of the world.

U.S. Special Forces, British SAS, and Royal Marine Commandos as well as other NATO elite forces would themselves be committed behind Warsaw Pact lines in case of war.

Despite the increasing sophistication of modern weaponry, elite forces show no sign of decreasing in importance. On the contrary, as weapons of mass destruction become more terrifying, the need for small groups of highly trained soldiers capable of carrying out surgical strikes becomes even more important. Elite counterterrorist units are also the answer to winning the war against terrorism. Giving in to terrorist demands certainly is not.

No matter how many dangerous and ingenious weapons are

conceived, the most dangerous is still man. The most sophisticated missile or bomb can malfunction or become obsolete, but the man wearing the beret, trained in silent mayhem, capable of taking the war to the enemy even in this own headquarters, will remain an awesome weapon in any country's arsenal. Unlike so much of society which is dedicated to the glorification of the anti-hero or the cult of the 'average', elite units are not trained for failure but for the successful accomplishment of their mission. Any U.S. airborne trooper knows the answer to the question, 'How far?' is 'All the way!' And, whether he serves in the SAS or the Soviet airborne commandos, the elite soldier instinctively and by training knows, 'Who Dares Wins!'

The Colour Plates and Plate Descriptions

1. Captain, 10th Special Forces Group

2. Special Forces Sergeant

3. Special Forces Master Sergeant

PLATE 1

4. Airborne Ranger

6. LRRP

5. Counterterrorist Commando

PLATE 2

7. Air Force Combat
   Security Policeman

8. 82nd Airborne –
   Private First Class

9. Air Force Pararescue
   Sergeant

PLATE 3

10. Navy SEAL (Vietnam)

11. Navy SEAL (Current)

12. Navy UD

PLATE 4

13. Marine Corps Officer

14. Marine Corps Drill Instructor

15. Marine Corps
Lance Corporal

PLATE 5

16. U.S. Marine Recon

18. British SAS Trooper

17. British SAS 'Tree Jumper'

PLATE 6

SAS Lieutenant Colonel

21. Paratrooper (Suez)

20. SAS Counterterrorist Commando

PLATE 7

22. Paratrooper (Current)

23. Royal Marine Commando

24. RAF Regiment
(Airborne) Corporal

PLATE 8

Royal Marine
Commando
(Ulster)

27. SBS Combat Swimmer

26. Royal Marine Commando
SBS Canoeist

PLATE 9

28. British SAS HALO Jumper

30. Italian Para Frogman

29. Italian 'San Marco' Marine

PLATE 10

31. Alpini Ski Trooper

33. Carabinieri Parachutist

32. Airborne Sergeant

PLATE 11

34. Airborne Feldwebel

36. GSG-9 Commander

35. GSG-9 Counterterrorist Commando

PLATE 12

37. Belgian Paratrooper

39. Greek Paratrooper

38. Portuguese Commando

PLATE 13

40. Canadian Airborne Staff Sergeant

42. Turkish Paratroop Sergeant

41. Dutch Marine Sergeant

PLATE 14

43. Airborne Private

44. Airborne Senior Sergeant

45. Airborne Sniper

PLATE 15

46. Airborne Sub-Lieutenant

48. Naval Infantry Senior Lieutenan

47. Naval Infantry Major

PLATE 16

49. Soviet Naval Infantry Commando

51. Polish Naval Infantry
    Battalion Sergeant Major

50. Polish Airborne 2nd Lieutenant

PLATE 17

52. Czech Paratroop Lance Corporal

53. Bulgarian Paratroop Corporal

54. East German Airborn
Regimental Lance
Corporal

PLATE 18

55. Hungarian
Paratrooper

57. Yugoslavian
Mountain
Trooper

56. Rumanian Paratroop Corporal

PLATE 19

58. Colonial
    Paratrooper

59. Paratroop Lieutenant Colonel

60. Foreign Legion
    Paratrooper

PLATE 20

Trooper,
11th Parachute Division

63. Naval Infantry Commando

62. Foreign Legion Paratroop Lieutenant

PLATE 21

64. Austrian
'Schlangenfresser'
Corporal

65. Swiss Grenadier Parachutist

66. Spanish
Paratroo
Private

PLATE 22

67. Australian
    SAS Trooper

69. Rhodesian Selous Scout (1978)

68. South African Recon Commando

PLATE 23

70. Paratroop Staff Sergeant

72. Para-Frogman

71. Paratroop Corporal

PLATE 24

73. Egyptian Incursor
    Commando

75. Lieutenant, Sultan of
    Oman's Special Force

74. Egyptian Paratrooper

PLATE 25

76. Iraqi Special Forces Trooper

77. Iranian Special Forces Trooper

78. Jordanian Paratroop
Lieutenant Colonel

PLATE 26

79. Indian Paratrooper

80. Indian Paratroop Lieutenant Colonel

81. Thai LRRP

PLATE 27

82. Chinese Republican Paratrooper

84. Republic of Vietnam Special Forces Commando

83. Nationalist Chinese Amphibious Commando

PLATE 28

85. Indonesian Police Mobile
    Brigade Sergeant 1st Class

87. Vietnamese Parachute Nurse

86. ROK Special Forces Trooper

PLATE 29

88. Chilean Special Forces
    Paratrooper

90. Panamanian National Guard
    Paratrooper

89. Japanese Airborne PFC

PLATE 30

91. Brazilian Paratrooper

93. Kenyan Paratroop Corporal

92. Brazilian Amphibious Recon Sergeant

PLATE 31

94. Zaire Paratroop Officer

96. Senegalese Paratrooper

95. Congolese Paratrooper

PLATE 32

1. NATO/USA: Captain 10th Special Forces Group – Current.

The U.S. Special Forces are descendants of the 1st Special Service Force and Rangers of World War II. Originally activated at Fort Bragg in 1952, the Special Forces were trained primarily in guerrilla warfare, but their mission has since evolved to include counterinsurgency, training and advising friendly troops, and counterterrorism. During the Vietnam War, members of the Special Forces led and trained indigenous Vietnamese troops and also carried out missions behind enemy lines such as the attempt to free POWs from Son Tay Prison.

All members of Special Forces are airborne qualified (many are also HALO and SCUBA trained) and also trained in at least two specialties such as intelligence, weapons, medical, communications, or demolitions and engineering. Each Special Forces trooper is highly qualified in his own specialty and cross trained in another. This dual training allows critical skills to be duplicated in each team in case its strength is split or a member becomes a casualty.

Training in a trooper's specialty is intensive:

COMMUNICATIONS: A Special Forces communications expert goes through 16 weeks of training during which time he learns to send and receive Morse at the rate of 18 words per minute, learns cryptography, and learns operation, repair and maintenance of transmitting and receiving equipment, generators, and antennas.

MEDICAL: A Special Forces medic goes through 37 to 50 weeks of training and is qualified to even perform field surgery in an emergency. Teaching hygiene and disease prevention to indigenous troops as well as giving them basic medical care is another task of the S.F. medic.

DEMOLITIONS AND ENGINEERING: This 8 week course trains the Special Forces trooper to blow up a bridge or build a dam depending upon the situation. Special emphasis is placed on the ability to create explosives devices from the materials available when conventional explosives are not available. Use of incendiaries is also stressed. Building skills are taught so that the engineering specialist can aid in a 'hearts and minds' campaign by helping indigs improve their villages, etc.

WEAPONS: The weapons specialist receives 8 weeks of training in both U.S. and foreign weapons. About one-third of this time is spent on mortars, while another one-third is spent on machine-guns, rifles, carbines, and shotguns. Submachine-guns, handguns, anti-tank weapons, tactical training, grenades, constructing firing ranges in the field, the history of small arms, and techniques to be used in teaching marksmanship take up the remainder of the training time.

OPERATIONS AND INTELLIGENCE: This 8 week course covers Tactical Terrain, Analysis, Fingerprinting, Order of Battle, Operational Planning, Photography, Cryptography, Clandestine Communications, Intelligence Nets, Methods of Interrogation, Organizing Guerrilla Units, and Psychological Warfare (known as 'Psy Ops').

The basic Special Forces operational unit is the 12 man A Team. The commanding officer of an A Team is normally a Captain, and the executive officer is normally a 1st Lieutenant. The remaining 10 men are Sergeants trained in the various specialties. Included in a normal team are an Operations Sergeant, a Heavy Weapons Leader, an Intelligence Sergeant, a Light Weapons Leader, a Medical Specialist, a Radio Operator Supervisor, an Engineer Sergeant, an Assistant Medical Specialist, a Research and Development Operator, and an Engineering Specialist.

Normally four A Teams are controlled by a B Detachment (Team) commanded by a Major. Three B Detachments plus an administrative detachment normally comprise a C Team or Special Forces Company commanded by a Lt. Colonel. Three or more of these companies or C Detachments, a signals company, and often an aviation detachment make up a Special Forces Group.

On his beret the officer illustrated wears the flash of the 10th Special Forces Group which is stationed in West Germany. The oval backing of his senior parachutist's badge also identifies him as a member of the 10th SFG. Note the colors of the Federal Republic of Germany on both the flash and the oval. Most members of the 10th SFG speak fluent German and are well accepted by the local population near their bases. During maneuvers they easily blend with the 'indigs' who supply them with information about the 'enemy'.

The bars designating this officer's rank are worn on his beret flash. Enlisted men wear the crossed arrow and dagger badge of the Special Forces on the flash. The Combat Infantryman's badge and ribbons (including the DSM, silver star, bronze star, Army Commendation Medal, AFE Medal, Vietnam Service Medal, *et. al.*) on his left breast and the Republic of Vietnam Jump Wings and U.S. Presidential Unit Citation on his right breast identify this officer as a veteran of the Vietnam War. Also on his right breast is the oak leaves and acorn badge identifying him as an 'Einzelkaempfer', a graduate of the West German Ranger program. Many Special Forces troops go through the elite or special training program of an allied country (reportedly a few on clandestine assignment have even gone through those of unfriendly countries). Members of the 10th SFG, for example, might choose to go through the 'Einzelkaempfer' training as did this captain or they might go through the German or Italian Alpine school. The 7th Special Forces troops who are stationed in Panama, on the other hand, would probably attend a South American training program such as Colombia's Lancero School.

The arrow patch of the Special Forces is worn at the shoulder along with the light blue airborne tab.

2. NATO/USA: U.S. Special Forces Sergeant, 'Project Delta' – Vietnam War.

This sergeant is part of a covert recon team launched from a Delta FOB (Forward Operating Base) or from a C & C FOB such as CCN (Command and Control North) at Da Nang. A part of Special Operations Group (SOG), DELTA recon teams were composed of two to three American Special Forces troops and three to six indigenous personnel. These teams undertook missions into Cambodia, Laos, and North Vietnam. The figure wears one of the camouflage patterns sometimes incorrectly called 'Tiger Stripes' (see Plate 4 for true 'Tiger Stripes') and popular with the Nungs and Montagnards fighting for the Special Forces as well as with their 'green beret' advisors. This four color (two greens, a brown, and a black) pattern came into use during 1968. Around his head this trooper wears a green bandanna, probably an olive drab bandage or piece of a towel. His load bearing harness is the STABO rig which was made in Taiwan for the CIA and Special Forces. The snap links at the shoulders allowed men to be lifted out of the jungle rapidly by helicopter while both arms remained free in case it was necessary to use one's weapons during a contested extraction. He wears standard jungle boots but without the canvas leggings sometimes worn by MACV/SOG troopers. Although this trooper carries a canteen on his pistol belt in front, common practice was to carry multiple canteens at back and mini-grenades and ammo pouches in front.

MACV/SOG troops were normally well armed, and this sergeant is no exception. On his STABO harness on the left side he wears the U.S. Air Force Pilot's Survival Knife, but Randall and PAL knives were also popular. The pistol is a silenced High Standard .22 automatic used to eliminate sentries or in any other situations requiring silent killing. The Special Forces also used crossbows for this purpose. His braced firing stance allows exact shot placement, a necessity with the small .22 round. Excellent accuracy out to 50 yards or better can be achieved from a braced position such as this with practice. Over his shoulder is slung the CAR-15 (XM177E2) short version of the M-16, but the Swedish K SMG was also popular with SOG troops. 'Clean' 9 mm. Browning Hi-power pistols untraceable to the U.S., Ithaca M37 12 gauge riot guns, silenced Sten guns, sawed off M-79 grenade launchers with anti-personnel loads, and the XM-203 version of the M-16 which had a 40 mm. grenade launcher mounted below the barrel were all used by DELTA teams at one time or another.

3. NATO/USA: U.S. Special Forces Master Sergeant – Vietnam War.

This sergeant wears the standard U.S. Army khaki uniform with

Special Forces arrowhead patch and black airborne tab. The flash on his green beret is of the 5th Special Forces Group. It incorporates the colors of the South Vietnamese flag. On the flash is the crossed arrows and dagger badge of the Special Forces which bears the motto 'De Oppresso Liber'. The oval behind his parachutist's wings also bears the colors of the 5th S.F.G. Trousers are bloused into his combat boots in accepted airborne style.

Although this trooper now appears to be assigned to a desk job, perhaps at the MACV/SOG headquarters on Pasteur Street in Saigon, the Vietnamese jump wings and U.S. Unit Citation on his right breast plus the combat infantryman's badge, bronze star ribbon, and purple heart ribbon on his left breast indicate he has seen his share of action. His coffee mug bears the MACV/SOG death's head-with-green beret-on shell burst insignia which, though not official, was sported on everything from coffee mugs to jockey shorts.

4. NATO/USA: U.S. Airborne Ranger – 1960.

In addition to being a trained paratrooper, the Airborne Ranger was and is a skilled mountaineer and jungle fighter. The Rangers trace their lineage to Rogers' Rangers of French and Indian War fame and to the U.S. Rangers of World War II. U.S. Airborne Rangers were used extensively during the Korean and Vietnam Wars for missions behind enemy lines (though in Vietnam the enemy rarely had 'lines'). Ranger training continues to be among the toughest in the U.S. armed forces. Lasting 58 grueling days, this training stresses physical endurance, mental alertness, patrolling, mountaineering and climbing, jungle and swamp survival, and small boat assault landings. Upon graduation, most Rangers return to their units of origin, but some of the top graduates may end up in one of the two crack Ranger battalions – the 1/75 or 2/75. Airborne Rangers assigned to these two battalions currently wear a black beret in addition to their Ranger tabs.

The Ranger illustrated wears standard fatigue cap and heavy winter fatigues with the collar turned up to protect his neck while using a rope when climbing or when parachuting. Note that his 'greenies' are tied close to his body so they do not get in his way while climbing or moving silently through the bush. Around his waist he carries a climbing rope, a piece of equipment the Rangers are well skilled in the use of.

His weapon is the M-14 7.62 mm. NATO rifle which was the standard U.S. service weapon between 1957 and 1964 when it was replaced by the M-16. Many feel the M-14 should have been retained because of its far more powerful round. Basically, the M-14 is an improved version of the World War II M-1 Garand but with selective fire option, an improved system of tapping gas to operate the action, and a 20 round detachable box magazine.

5. NATO/USA: U.S. Special Forces Sergeant – Operational Group – Delta, Current.

Operational Group – Delta is the U.S. counterterrorist unit which is stationed at Fort Bragg, North Carolina. Members of Delta Group are airborne qualified and have been through a rigorous selection and training program. All are experts in hand-to-hand combat and marksmanship. This trooper is dressed for a field operation and wears camouflage utilities and bush hat. His weapon is the M60 GPMG which at about $10\frac{1}{2}$ kg is heavy for easy use in counterterrorist operations. Still, it is an excellent weapon for giving suppressive fire. Its 550 RPM cyclic rate (200 RPM practical full auto rate) is low enough so it can be easily controlled and skilled users can carry the M60 in the assault position as illustrated and get off surprisingly accurate aimed bursts. Delta members also use Remington 700–7.62 mm. sniper's rifles, M-16s, CAR-15s, M-3s and other SMGs, and M-79 or M-203 40 mm. grenade launchers. All members of Delta Group carry a highly accurized Colt .45 automatic pistol with which they practise almost daily. This sergeant has added Pachmayr rubber grips to improve the 'feel' of his .45. These grips will not slip even in a wet or perspiring hand. He also uses an open holster instead of a flapped type to allow faster access to his weapon.

In addition to continuous training in use of their own weapons, members of Delta Group spend a great deal of time practising with foreign weapons likely to be encountered in the hands of terrorists and in undertaking practice rescue missions in all types of environments.

6. NATO/USA: LRRP (Long Range Reconnaissance Patrol) – Vietnam War.

Many LRRPs (pronounced 'Lurps') were trained at the MACV Recondo School run by the Special Forces at Nha Trang. LRRPs were airborne qualified and trained to operate behind enemy lines gathering information about enemy movement and dispositions. The LRRP tried to avoid contact if possible, relying on stealth rather than firepower.

The LRRP illustrated wears camouflage utilities along with matching bush hat. Around his neck is an OD towel. His standard load bearing rig is the M-56 H-harness/pistol belt combination with lightweight rucksack. The LRRP was normally festooned with canteens. Some LRRPs carried six or eight canteens because their freeze-dried Long Range Patrol rations required a large amount of liquid. Also, they often operated in areas where drinking water was hard to obtain, since the enemy was likely to control most sources of fresh water. Ready for instant use he carries M26A1 grenades taped to the ammo pouches at his waist. Smoke grenades such as the one on his left breast, claymore mines, M34 'Willie Pete' grenades, explosives and demolition cord were also normally carried. Though the LRRP was normally not on raiding missions he was prepared to blow up juicy targets of opportunity. Note that even his M-16 rifle has been camouflaged and has had the swivels removed to prevent them from making noise. Up to thirty magazines of ammunition were often carried for the M-16 in universal pouches and bandoliers since if the LRRP were discovered by the enemy he needed enough ammo to hold off attackers until a lift-out chopper could arrive. Attached to this figure's right suspender is the M7 knife bayonet, but the usual range of Ka-Bars, Jet Pilot's survival knives, and Randalls or Gerbers were also used by the LRRPs.

7. NATO/USA: U.S. Air Force Combat Security Policeman – Vietnam War.

The Combat Security Police were an elite Air Force strike unit trained to aggressively defend U.S. air bases by mounting small unit patrols and ambushes on the outskirts of the bases. CSPs received training similar to the Army's Rangers, with special emphasis on weapons use and hand-to-hand combat. The mere presence of a Combat Security Police squadron on a U.S. air base was usually sufficient to discourage any VC or NVA infiltrators.

This Combat Security Policeman wears camouflage to allow him to blend into the scrub and elephant grass which surrounded most air bases. When not out on a sweep or an ambush, he would be likely to wear the dark blue beret originally awarded to the first Combat Security Police graduates of the 'Safeside' Program. In addition to his S & W Model 15 .38 Special revolver he carries the Remington 870 slide action 12 gauge riot gun. This was a very popular close quarters weapon with all combat personnel in Vietnam. The Special Forces favored the Ithaca 12 gauge fighting shotgun, while many Marines still used the Model 12 Winchesters which had been in their inventory since World War II or earlier. In addition to shotguns, the Combat Security Police also used the M-16, CAR-15, M-79 40 mm. grenade launcher, and M60 GPMG with deadly effect.

8. NATO/USA: 82nd Airborne – Private First Class – Current.

This paratrooper wears the experimental desert camouflage pattern which is appropriate to the 82nd Airborne's possible role in the Rapid Deployment Force. He also wears the maroon beret which after a period of two years when it was not authorized for wear was re-instated in the 82nd at the end of 1980. Beret flash and/or crest will vary among sub units of the Division. Jungle boots are worn in preference to the normal black jump boots because of their suitability in hot climates.

The subdued divisional patch of the 82nd 'All American' Airborne and subdued airborne tab are worn. Subdued rank insignia are worn on the collar. His weapon is the standard M-16. Though he is not 'chuted up', this paratrooper would use the MC1-1B steerable parachute for a combat jump. All personnel assigned to the 82nd Airborne are jump qualified including the female soldiers in the division.

9. NATO/USA: U.S. Air Force Pararescue Sergeant – Current.

The USAF Pararescue Service is one of the world's least known elite forces. Charged with rescuing downed aircrew on sea or land, often behind enemy lines and under fire, airmen of the pararescue service are airborne qualified and scuba trained. They also receive medical, ranger, and survival training, making them among the most versatile fighting men in the world. Four points of attire set this pararescueman apart. Most noticeable is his maroon beret with the Pararescue badge bearing the motto, 'That Others Might Live'. The jump wings on his left breast and the bloused trousers with combat boots identify him as a paratrooper, while the aircrewman's wings above the parachutist's wings designate that he is on flight status. His four stripes identify him as a staff sergeant.

10. NATO/USA: U.S. Navy SEAL, Vietnam War.

The U.S. Navy SEAL (Sea Air Land for the elements he is trained to operate in) is an expert combat swimmer, skilled in techniques of open, semi-closed, and closed circuit SCUBA. All SEALs are paratroopers, and many are HALO specialists. Some SEALs are also specially trained for underwater operations in the Arctic. In addition to demolitions training in the use of the limpet mine and other explosives, the SEAL learns skills applicable to the land portion of his mission. He becomes highly proficient in the use of small arms, many of which are unique to the SEALs, and in the martial art Hwarang Do which stresses use of the knife and club as well as unarmed techniques.

This Vietnam era SEAL has probably just landed from a small boat in the Mekong Delta region and is equipped to set an ambush along the Viet Cong trail network through this swampy area. He wears 'Tiger Stripes' camouflage clothing and face paint. His weapon is the Stoner M63A1 Light Machine-Gun favored by the SEALs. The 5.56 mm. Stoner was light (12.5 lbs. unloaded) and with the 150 round drum magazine illustrated gave the SEALs a lot of firepower. Additional ammunition is carried in belts around this figure's torso. The Stoner was not 'soldier proof' and had a tendency to malfunction when used by conventional units, but the SEALs carefully maintained their weapons, and despite its tendency to go full auto at inopportune times, they found the M63A1 a highly satisfactory weapon.

11. NATO/USA: U.S. Navy SEAL – Current.
Currently the U.S. Navy maintains SEAL Team One at Coronada, California and SEAL Team Two at Little Creek, Virginia. Both are ready to undertake combat assignments as needed but are also charged with the recovery of U.S. space vehicles at sea.

This SEAL is equipped for a beach incursion, possibly to survey enemy defenses. His inflatable life vest and diving mask are the standard issue items for both the SEALs and UDTs. Since he wears only the wetsuit top with trunks on the bottom he is probably not operating in Northern waters. His weapon is the U.S. Navy Mark 22, Model 0 silenced 9 mm. pistol manufactured by Smith & Wesson for the SEALs. This weapon is fabricated of stainless steel so it will not rust in salt water. Known as the 'Hush Puppy' because it was intended for use against enemy guard dogs, this pistol also saw extensive use against human enemies in Vietnam. Utilizing a slide lock to keep the action closed while firing and special sub-sonic 9 mm. ammunition, the 'Hush Puppy' is an extremely effective silent killer. A special oversized holster is also worn so that the 'Hush Puppy' may be carried with the silencer affixed, ready to be used instantly and silently as the SEAL rises from the sea on an unfriendly beach. Also on his pistol belt this figure carries the U.S. Navy Underwater Knife.

12. NATO/USA: U.S. Navy UDT 'Frogman' – Current.

The U.S. Navy UDT (Underwater Demolition Team) or 'Frogman' undergoes the same SCUBA and airborne training as the SEAL, but once he joins his operational team he specializes more exclusively in the skills of underwater combat. This UDT wears twin SCUBA tanks which allow him to stay underwater long enough to complete his mission. 'Twin-80s', double 80 cubic feet capacity aluminum tanks, are commonly used. If a closed circuit air system is worn, no bubbles will escape to the surface to betray his presence. Both UDTs and SEALs are trained to 'lock in and out' of submerged submarines and are also skilled at high speed techniques of entering and exiting the water via high speed boats or helicopters. In addition to these 'casting' techniques, both SEALs and UDTs can drop through the enemy radar net using HALO techniques, opening their parachutes for only the last few seconds of their descents. Upon hitting the water, the parachute can either be jettisoned or collapsed and sunk. The swimmer then proceeds to the enemy shore under water.

This UDT wears a full wetsuit and carries his flippers. In his hand is the U.S. Navy Underwater Knife used by both the UDTs and SEALs. All metal parts of this knife are made of rust resistant non-ferrous metals. It can be carried on the arm as this frogman carries his, on the leg, or at the belt. One edge of the blade has saw teeth, while the other is a normal cutting edge.

13. NATO/USA: U.S. Marine Corps First Lieutenant – Current.

This Lieutenant wears the distinctive Marine Corps blues. This is the same basic uniform worn by embassy guards and Marine guards aboard cruisers and aircraft carriers. This is the normal USMC dress uniform, though a number one or 'Mess' dress exists for formal wear. The cap badge and collar insignia are the eagle, globe, and anchor. The Sam Browne belt and shoes are highly polished. Not having served during the Vietnam War, this officer has only peacetime ribbons such as the National Defense Service Medal and Good Conduct Medal. Unlike the U.S. Army, Air

Force, and Navy, the Marine Corps does not have its own service academy from which to draw officers. Annapolis gradutes can elect to serve in the Marines instead of the Navy, but the primary source of officers is through the PLC (Platoon Leaders Class), Naval ROTC, or OCS (Officers Candidate School). In each case the Marine officer, including Annapolis graduates, goes through a rigorous training and selection process at Quantico before commissioning. All Marines, including officers, are basically combat infantrymen and are trained as such. That is why Marine Corps support personnel have traditionally fought like front line troops when necessary.

14. NATO/USA: U.S. Marine Corps Drill Instructor – Current.

The drill instructor is the real backbone of the Corps, and his campaign hat, blood curdling stare, and clenched teethed growl all identify him as the man who turns civilian 'maggots' (and that should be read with disgust in one's voice) into Marines in 11 weeks of boot camp. At a time when other branches of the U.S. armed forces were showing recruiting films emphasizing how pleasant their branch was, the Marine Corps recruiting films showed a drill instructor putting boots through agonizing physical training, while the song 'I Never Promised You a Rose Garden' played in the background.

Most Marines would never want to go through boot camp a second time, but they know they are far better prepared to survive in combat because of it. Few can imagine an enemy more ferocious than a Leatherneck DI. This staff sergeant's short sleeve uniform shirt is especially well-suited to the heat and humidity at the two USMC recruit depots -- San Diego, California and Parris Island, South Carolina. In true DI fashion, this figure manages to look cool and 'squared away' even after hours of drill. The general rumor is that DIs have their sweat glands removed upon receipt of the 'Smokey the Bear' hat.

15. NATO/USA: U.S. Marine Corps Lance Corporal – Current.

This lance corporal wears the new camouflage adopted by the Corps and carries the M-16 rifle. On his webbed belt he wears the USMC 'Ka-Bar' fighting/utility Bowie style knife. As a Marine infantryman assigned to the Fleet Marine Force, he could be slated to serve in the Rapid Deployment Force. In the Marine Corps, there are two corporal's ranks. One chevron over crossed rifles as worn by this Marine denotes a lance corporal, while two chevrons over the rifles indicates full corporal's rank. This figure is moving in the most accepted Marine Corps manner, at the double time.

16. NATO/USA: U.S. Marine Corps Recon – Current.

The Recon is an elite within the already elite ranks of the U.S. Marine Corps. A Recon has been through up to two years of intensive training to earn him this special status. During this training, he becomes airborne qualified and is often skilled at HALO (High Altitude Low Opening) jumps. Additionally, he is a trained combat swimmer. Other training includes Forward Air Controlling, Artillery Observing, demolitions, photography, map reading, patrolling, and extensive polishing of hand-to-hand combat skills. Although all Marines receive excellent small arms training, the Recon polishes his weapons skills even further, learning the use of foreign as well as U.S. arms. To top off this other training, many Recons are trained as Rangers.

All of this training is put to use operating behind enemy lines, often to call in air or artillery strikes, scouting enemy beaches in preparation for amphibious landings, and undertaking any other special mission required of the Recons. The basic Recon unit is the four man squad. Each Marine division has a Recon battalion with a strength of around 500 men. There are also Force Recon companies assigned directly to the commander of a Marine Amphibious Force.

The Recon Marine illustrated wears the same type of flotation vest used by the Navy's UDTs and SEALs. Prepared for a night mission, his face is covered with grease paint camouflage which also makes an effective sun screen during the day. Quite often a rope is carried to allow the four men of the squad to keep contact while swimming under water. This Recon's weapon is the M-16 with M-203 40 mm. grenade luncher attached. Standard knife for the Recons is the USMC Ka-Bar, but many prefer to carry a Randall or Gerber.

17. NATO/UK: British Special Air Service Trooper – Malaya – 1952.

The fight against Communist terrorists in Malaya graphically illustrated the need for special units like the SAS which was reinstated as a regular formation in 1952 after having been relegated to Territorial status after World War II. The Malayan Scouts (a hodgepodge of former SAS members as well as troops from assorted other units) and elements of the Territorial Army's 21st SAS (Artists) were amalgamated into the 22nd SAS Regiment. (Those readers who may be curious about the history of the other twenty SAS Regiments, will be interested to know that the '2' and '1' of 21st SAS represent the war-time 1st and 2nd SAS Regiments in reverse order; the War Office humorists at the time for some reason finding it easier for the records to call the new Regular Regiment – the '22nd'; one other TA SAS Regiment came into existence in the late 1950s and by simple arithmetical progression and maybe to further mislead Britain's enemies as to the strength of the SAS was called – the '23rd'.) In Malaya the SAS readily adapted to conditions in the jungle, proving themselves excellent trackers able to follow the CTs to their lairs deep in the jungle. Among the special counterguerrilla tactics developed by the SAS in Malaya, one of the most interesting was 'tree-jumping'.

Because of the thick canopy over Southeast Asian rain forests, normal dropping zones for parachute jumps were not available; hence, the SAS learned to jump directly on to the trees. Theoretically, the chute's canopy would catch on the matted tree tops, and the trooper would lower himself to the ground with the rope he carried.

The figure illustrated is fitted out for a 'tree jump'. He wears the maroon beret with the traditional winged dagger badge which replaced the short-lived Artists Rifles 'Mars and Minerva' badge of the 21st SAS (Artists) in 1949. The maroon Airborne Division beret was superseded in the late 1950s when the SAS retrieved its autonomous status, as well, by the original and current sand colored one. The uniform is the standard olive green one worn in the jungle with a sleeveless smock over it. Puttees are wrapped over the rubber and canvas jungle boots and up to the top of the calf to protect the jumper's legs from branches while penetrating the trees and to give ankle support during landings on hard ground. At his feet are a standard paratrooper's helmet and his Bergen rucksack, which was preferred by the SAS to the Airborne Kitbag in service at that time. For the jump, the frame was removed from the Bergen and replaced loosely with the curve of the frame inwards. Both Bergen and frame were then wrapped in a simple canvas cover; the bundle being secured by rope to one of the lower cross straps of the parachute harness and hung upside down by two release hooks clipped on to two D-rings attached to the upper two cross straps. This valise device was invented by an SAS sergeant during the Malayan Emergency and used by the SAS for many years afterwards. The rope for lowering himself from the trees is carried over his abdomen, while just visible below the rope on his right hip is the holster of his Browning 9 mm. automatic pistol. The pistol was issued for use in case CTs were encountered while the jumper was still in his parachute harness and unable to reach his main armament. (It should be noted that pistols and revolvers have always been widely coveted by airborne troops for just such emergencies, whatever the regulations.) This trooper's primary armament would probably be the Sten 9 mm. SMG or the .303 No. 4 MK1 Rifle or No.5 MK1 Jungle Carbine, though Browning twelve gauge semi-automatic shotguns were also widely used in the jungle.

18. NATO/UK: British SAS Trooper – Aden, 1964
With his improvised desert headdress, goggles, and beard, this

member of the SAS almost looks like a throwback to his World War II progenitors who served under David Stirling in the Western Desert. Even his windproof smock is a familiar SAS item, having remained in service since the early days. He wears standard khaki drill trousers, but the desert boots, though popular because of their suitability for operations in Aden, are not standard. His binoculars and flat-shooting L1A1 7.62 mm. SLR were especially well-suited to operations in Aden's mountainous Radfan.

Though this SAS trooper is attired and equipped for 'conventional' counterguerrilla operations, other members of the SAS fought a clandestine 'Keeni-Meeni' campaign in the more populous parts of Aden dressed as natives. Supposedly ability with the Browning Hi-Power pistol was a prime prerequisite for such assignments.

Although this figure has been described as a 'trooper', it is more likely that he is an officer, badges of rank not being worn on operational duty. Clues revealing his probable commissioned status are the pipe – a habit adopted mainly by the officers –, the binoculars and the sandboots, which other ranks would be frowned upon for wearing.

19. NATO/UK: British Special Air Service Lieutenant Colonel – Current.

This officer wears the standard khaki No. 2 dress uniform with silver buttons. The sand colored beret was re-instituted for SAS wear in 1957, having been replaced in 1944 prior to D-Day by the maroon beret of the airborne forces. (In 1944 the SAS Brigade was assigned to the First Allied Airborne Army but the SAS never enjoyed its association with the 'Red Devils.') The original sand colored beret worn during World War II was meant to blend with the surroundings in North Africa and offer a certain amount of camouflage. (Photographs also exist of SAS troopers wearing white berets in 1941.) The SAS winged dagger badge – raised in the case of an officer – is worn on the beret, and SAS parachutist's wings are on the right arm. Metal winged dagger badges are worn on the lapels. Black leather gloves and Sam Browne belt are worn. From this officer's ribbons, it is obvious he has seen his share of combat. As a Lieutenant Colonel and Commanding Officer, he wears a single star and crown on his shoulders. The three SAS Regiments are commanded by Lieutenant Colonels. One officer of higher rank exists in the SAS – a Brigadier who supervises the affairs of 21st, 22nd and 23rd SAS.

20. NATO/UK: British Special Air Service CRW Counter-Terrorist Commando – Iranian Embassy, London, May, 1980.

Because of the high level of training given to all SAS Troopers, each is considered capable of functioning in the counter-terrorist role, and squadrons alternate in serving in the CRW (Counter Revolutionary Warfare) counter-terrorist capacity. For years the SAS carried out this mission in relative obscurity, but in May, 1980, the whole world became aware of the SAS as a potent counter-terrorist force. Storming the Iranian Embassy in London during 'Operation Nimrod' and killing all but one of the terrorists who had begun executing their hostages, the SAS once again proved that 'Who Dares Wins'.

This CRW assault trooper wears a uniform which has been dyed black to enable him to blend into the shadows. His gray anti-flash hood protects him from the blast of explosives and along with his respirator gives him a fearsome unworldly appearance which might cause a terrorist to hesitate a critical second in shock. The mask and respirator also help disguise the CRW trooper's identity. In addition, the respirator serves the more mundane purpose of protecting him from CS gas. Under the hood he wears radio equipment which allows him to remain in contact with other members of his unit. His black flak vest will protect him from most handgun or submachine gun rounds, though a hit on the torso would still normally render him *hors de combat*. He is firing his 14 round (1 in the chamber and 13 in the magazine) Browning Hi-Power 9 mm. pistol which when not in use would be carried in the open 'combat' holster on his right hip. His black gloves protect his hands while abseiling down a rope, smashing in windows, etc. In his left hand is a magnesium based 'flash, bang' stun grenade, the blast of which will incapacitate terrorists for a matter of seconds, enough time for the CRW trooper to sort out the terrorists and 'neutralize' them. Though not visible, this CRW trooper would also normally be armed with the Heckler & Koch MP5 9 mm. SMG.

The skill of the SAS assault group with their Browning automatics is outstanding, and this trooper's instinctive firing crouch is entirely consistent with his training. He has been trained to instantly identity friend or foe and score hits on his target's head while running or tumbling into a room. This skill is developed through intensive training in the SAS Close Quarters Battle House (sometimes called the 'Killing House'). This house, which in U.S. combat shooting terminology would be called a 'Fun House', is designed to allow the SAS trooper to become an expert marksman, to instantly identify targets (photos of hostages were studied before the embassy raid so they could be instantly identified even in the heat of battle), to unhesitatingly make the split-second decision to shoot or not to shoot, to rapidly score two quick head or chest hits (head shots are necessary when a terrorist is shielded behind a hostage), to continually move while firing to avoid return fire, to perform fast magazine changes, and to clear jams or other malfunctions instantly. During this comprehensive training program, thousands of rounds of ammunition will be expended to perfect the CRW trooper's combat shooting skills. In addition to training in the CQB House, realistic exercises are also set up in mock ups of airliners, oil rigs, trains, or any other potential terrorist target.

The figure illustrated is from the CRW assault group, but there are other SAS counter-terrorist specialists who make up the containment group which cordons off the area occupied by the terrorists. Many of these troopers are expert snipers who can 'take out' a terrorist at long range if the 'shoot' order is given.

21. NATO/UK: British Paratrooper – Suez, 1956.

This paratrooper waiting to board his Valetta or Hastings is a member of the 3d Parachute Battalion Group, 16th Independent Parachute Brigade, which jumped to seize Gamil Airport on 5 November 1956. On his head is the maroon beret traditionally worn by British airborne forces. The beret badge is that of the Parachute Regiment. His Denison smock and denim trousers were typical of the airborne forces at the time. Boots are the standard Army issue boots with Commando soles and puttees are worn over the ankles. As the unit emplaned in Cyprus, the life jacket was worn as a standard RAF regulation for flying over the sea. (It proved to be a very useful cushion if the paratrooper bumped the back of his head on landing on the drop zone.) In his left hand is his helmet which will be worn for the actual jump but which will probably be replaced in combat by the beret. The parachute is the Irvin X-type. At his feet is his leg bag containing his kit. Bren guns and rifles would have been carried separately in a green felt valise, released in mid-air on a rope after jerking out two pins. (The ankle pin was the most difficult to release as it often meant bending over to give it a good tug.) The Sten 9 mm. SMG would have been broken up, *i.e.* the butt removed, and carried inside the upper cross straps of the parachute harness. The 9 mm. Brownings, issued to officers, senior NCOs and signallers, was conveniently stuffed in a large inside pocket of the smock. Though reserve chutes were available for the Suez jump, most paratroopers preferred to jump in time-honored British fashion with only one chute, feeling extra ammunition would be far more valuable than a second parachute. After the Suez jump, however, use of the reserve chute became the norm.

22. NATO/UK: Parachute Regiment Private – Current.

The distinctive red beret bearing the winged parachute with lion and crown badge and camouflage smock identify this trooper as one of the 'Red Devils' of the Parachute Regiment. His shoulder insignia indicates he is a member of the Territorial Army's London based 10th Parachute Battalion. Lightly equipped for patrolling, this paratrooper carries the L7A2 7.62 mm. General Purpose Machine-Gun with attached bipod. The L7A2 is the British version of the FN MAG, and in the form illustrated weighs almost 11 kg. Cyclic rate is 750–1000 RPM, but in LMG mode such as this, the maximum practical rate of fire is probably 100 rounds per minute.

23. NATO/UK: Royal Marine Commando – Current.

In addition to receiving mountain and ski training, Royal Marine Commandos are highly skilled in amphibious assault and air-mobile assault tactics, including assaults under Arctic conditions. Should NATO and the Warsaw Pact go to war, Royal Marine Commandos would be used in their traditional role as raiders along the Polish, E. German, and Soviet coastlines.

This Commando wears white snow camouflage and skis, equipping him for combat in the far north, possibly in Norway where Royal Marine Commandos could be committed in support of NATO operations. Note that this Commando's L1A1 rifle has also been camouflaged and that he uses his ski poles as a bipod while his left hand steadies the poles. As the Finns proved during their Winter War against the Soviet Union, snipers on skis can inflict heavy casualties against far superior forces by shooting and then fading away across the snow. Although telescopic sights such as the Trilux night scope are available for the semi-automatic L1A1, the consistently high standards of marksmanship among the Royal Marine Commandos (and all British military units for that matter) should make them effective even with open sighted rifles such as the one illustrated at this type of hit and run sniping.

24. NATO/UK: RAF Regiment, 2 Squadron (Airborne) Corporal – Current.

In 1962, 2 Squadron of the RAF Regiment was trained to function in the airborne commando role, all members of this squadron becoming qualified as parachutists. There are also small numbers of airborne qualified troops assigned to the other squadrons of the RAF Regiment, but only 2 Squadron is considered a parachute squadron. Though part of the Royal Air Force, the RAF Regiment is trained to fight as light infantry and has impressive combat credentials, having seen post World War II action in Palestine, Malaya, Suez, Borneo, Aden, Cyprus, Oman, and Northern Ireland.

This corporal wears his dress uniform with white belt, white rifle sling, and white gloves, indicating that he is probably standing ceremonial guard duty at Buckingham Palace, the Tower of London, or elsewhere. He might also be part of an honor guard. His regimental tab, parachutist's wings, and corporal's chevrons are worn on his upper arm. His weapon is the L1A1 7.62 mm. rifle with 20 round magazine in place.

25. NATO/UK: Royal Marine Commando – Ulster, 1975.

The Royal Marine Commandos are still one of the world's most highly skilled and highly respected elite forces. When it comes to amphibious raids or assaults up rocky coastal cliffs there are few who can match them. Although it is not really their 'cup of tea', the Royal Marine Commandos have also done their time on urban security duty in Ulster.

This Commando is equipped for street patrol in Belfast or another city. On his head is the most famous of all berets – the green one of the Commandos. He also wears the well-known Commando sweater with 'Royal Marines Commando' tab and parachutist's badge on the sleeve. It should be noted that his parachutist's wings mark him as one of the approximately 10 per cent of the Commandos who are parachute qualified. Over his sweater he wears a 'flak' vest to offer some protection from grenades or small arms fire.

Since he is on street patrol this Commando has his eyes and his L1A1 rifle pointed in the right direction – the rooftops where an IRA sniper might be lurking.

26. NATO/UK: Royal Marine Commando Special Boat Squadron Canoeist – Current.

The Special Boat Squadron based at Poole, Dorset is the British equivalent of the U.S. SEALs or USMC Recons. The SBS performs combat swimming/frogman missions and also beach reconnaissance. SBS members are selected from the already highly qualified Royal Marine Commandos and given an additional 20 weeks of training in parachuting, reconnaissance, demolitions, diving, and use of the Klepper canoe or Gemini. Additional training may follow after operational service with an SBS unit.

This SBS canoeist wears a waterproof smock and his green beret while silently paddling ashore on a raiding mission. His face and hands are camouflaged. Using the paddle silently is an art which allows SBS canoeists to glide into a beach without a sound. The canoe is also so close to the surface of the water that it is hard to detect on radar. His weapon, probably the silenced 9 mm. Sterling (L34A1) SMG, is inside the canoe. Chances are good that he also carries a fighting knife.

Although the SAS is normally charged with counterterrorist responsibility, reportedly SBS units are trained to respond to terrorist threats to North Sea oil rigs or to British ships. In any case, there is quite a bit of cooperation between the SAS and the SBS.

27. NATO/UK: RM Special Boat Squadron Combat Swimmer – Current.

This SBS frogman is chuted up and prepared for a 'wet jump' into the ocean. He wears his black rubberized underwater suit but has his hood turned up over his head. He carries his mask and fins. SBS swimmers prefer to use a 'dry suit' and closed circuit SCUBA gear so that no revealing bubbles are released.

Favorite weapons among SBS swimmers are the silenced Sterling (L34A1) SMG and the Browning Hi-Power 9 mm. pistol. There have been some reports that SBS swimmers also have silenced pistols but whether they use the same silenced S & W 9 mm. as the U.S. SEALs or have another weapon is not clear.

28. NATO/UK: British SAS Trooper in HALO Gear – 1977.

HALO (High Altitude Low Opening) parachute techniques are

especially well suited to units like the SAS or the U.S. Special Forces since small teams of men on incursion missions can quickly free fall off of enemy radar screens before deploying their chutes. SAS HALO troops undergo a six week HALO course which entails about 40 descents. The initial jump is from 12,000 feet but by the end of the course jumps are from 25,000 feet. Oxygen masks are normally required when jumping from 17,500 feet or above. Since operational HALO missions usually take place at night, night drops are stressed in training. In most respects, U.S. HALO training is quite similar to that of the SAS.

Before any jumps are made, a substantial amount of time is spent by the fledgling HALO jumpers learning proper body positioning for remaining stable in the arched back, spread eagled, face-to-ground, 'starfish' position necessary for military free falling. HALO free fallers usually reach a velocity of 120 mph before deploying their chutes which makes retention of body symmetry especially important. Deployment is normally at around 4,000 feet since at that height the sound of the chute opening is not audible from the ground. The weight carried by an SAS HALO jumper – often 100 lbs or more – makes perfect technique even more of a necessity.

When jumping from the higher altitudes, frostbite or ice on the goggles and altimeter can also be problems. Despite its dangers, HALO is considered a valuable technique by the SAS who have used HALO jumps on more than one occasion operationally, the best known probably being the insertion of a recon troop into Oman during 1970.

His oxygen mask and small oxygen bottle indicate the figure illustrated is dressed for a high altitude jump. His altimeter – very important since it can be difficult to judge when to pop one's chute while free falling, especially at night – is attached to his reserve chute, where he can readily see it from the 'starfish' position. His rucksack is worn below his main chute, a position which has been chosen because it offers the best weight distribution and least likelihood of shifting. Normal SAS camo smock and trousers are worn, though radar absorbent clothing is also available for operational jumps. Note also his thick soled jump boots, gloves (remember the danger of frostbite), and protective helmet. His weapon is the standard L1A1 rifle, but the U.S. M-16 is also popular with SAS HALO jumpers because of its light weight and the greater amount of its lighter ammo which may be carried. (Though it should be noted that the SAS normally considers far less ammunition sufficient than equivalent U.S. troops deem necessary.)

29. NATO/Italy: Italian Marine of the 'San Marco' Battalion – 1974.

The 'San Marco' Battalion is the elite formation of the Italian Marines. Its members are not only trained for amphibious assault but are also trained for airborne operations.

This Marine wears the easily recognizable Italian camouflage uniform with matching cover on his helmet. Although the life vest indicates he is taking part in an amphibious operation, he is lightly equipped with only his BM-59 rifle and the magazine pouch and bayonet on his belt.

When in non-battledress, members of the San Marco Battalion wear collar insignia consisting of a golden winged lion on red background. Some Marines also wear a black beret.

30. NATO/Italy: Italian Para Frogman – 1966.

Although combat swimmers have been used since ancient times, Italy's Naval Assault Divisions in World Wars I and II were among the pioneers of modern underwater warfare. At Trieste, Pola, Suda Bay, Alexandria, Gibraltar, and Malta, Italian frogmen proved their courage, skill, and the viability of combat swimmers in modern warfare.

Currently, the Incursori undergo a ten month training program at La Spezia which includes Ranger (especially scaling techniques), parachute, hand-to-hand, demolitions, and weapons training as well as constant gymnastic and physical training – all these in addition to SCUBA and other swimming skills. Theoretical knowledge is also considered important in such areas as topography, navigation, immersion physics, communications, and first aid. After graduation, the Italian frogman is assigned to an Operational Division.

This Incursori is dressed for a parachute jump into the water and wears his wet suit with diver's watch and fins. Note the very practical knee pads built into his suit. Although no weapon is visible, the compact Beretta 9 mm. Model 12 SMG is popular with the Incursori.

31. NATO/Italy: Italian Alpini Ski Trooper – Current.
Italy maintains five Alpini brigades ('Tridentina', 'Orobica', 'Iuwa', 'Cadore', and 'Tauninense'), each composed of a mountain infantry regiment, a fortress battalion, a signals company, an engineer company, a Carabinieri platoon, a mountain artillery regiment, and other support units. Assorted snow tractors, motor sledges, and helicopters lend mobility to these elite mountain units, but the individual ski trooper remains the Alpini brigades' basic essential element just as the mule remains an essential prime mover. Within each Alpini brigade, there is also a para-ski platoon whose members are airborne qualified.

This ski trooper wears the white Alpini winter uniform which grants both warmth and camouflage in the snow. The jacket has a hood which fits tightly around the face for warmth, though this trooper has his hood thrown back. Heavy white gloves are also worn. He wears black ski boots, but climbing boots are also issued. The traditional Alpini mountaineer's hat with black feather is worn with snow goggles, the latter a necessity for preventing snow blindness. Over his shoulders he carries skis and poles suitable for cross-country skiing, while slung over his back is the 7.62 mm. NATO BM59 Ital Alpini rifle which has a folding stock, pistol grip, and winter trigger which allows it to be fired while wearing gloves.

32. NATO/Italy: Italian Airborne Sergeant – Current.
Italian airborne forces can trace their lineage back to 1938 when the first Italian parachute battalion was formed, and the present

'Folgore' Parachute Brigade carries on this tradition in fine style, its ranks containing parachute troops trained as airborne Alpine troops, airborne commandos, airborne artillerymen, and other specialists.

The sergeant illustrated wears the maroon beret of the Parachute Brigade with the parachutist's beret badge. The Italian parachutist's camouflage uniform he wears is one of the most practical for airborne troops, having built in knee and elbow pads and being gathered at wrists, ankles, and waist. The camouflage pattern is the standard one in use with the Italian armed forces. On a brassard or 'hanger' at the left shoulder he wears the patch of the 'Folgore' Brigade and his sergeant's chevrons. Webbed belt and brown combat boots complete his attire.

Italian parachute troops wear their parachutist's badges on their right breast when they are worn. Members of the 'Folgore' Brigade may also be seen wearing collar insignia consisting of a silver 'Savoy' star and winged parachute with dagger. The color of the background the star rests on indicates function within the Brigade as follows: medium blue – all members of the Brigade except specialists, black with gold edging – artillery, black with red edging – engineers, royal blue with maroon border – signals, maroon – medical, purple – equipment supply, pale blue – food supply, black with royal blue border – administration.

The figure illustrated is armed with the BM59 Ital Para, the folding stock 'Paracadutisti' version of the standard service rifle. This 7.62 mm. NATO rifle is a development of the World War II U.S. M1 Garand, but with selective fire option and a 20 round detachable box magazine. The Para version of the rifle illustrated has a detachable grenade launcher. Note also that it is equipped with folding bipod.

33. NATO/Italy: Italian Carabinieri Parachutist – Current.
The Carabinieri Parachute Battalion is incorporated into the 'Folgore' Brigade, but also retains a certain amount of autonomy under the Carabinieri GHQ. The Carabinieri are a militarized national police force who also fulfill the military police function

for the Italian armed forces. Members of the Carabinieri Parachute Battalion act as MPs for the 'Folgore' Brigade, though this is not their sole duty. There are also indications that Italy's counter terrorist unit, the 50 man Squadron Anti-Commando, is drawn from the Carabinieri, and the Parachute Battalion would be the most likely unit to recruit them from.

This figure wears the standard Carabinieri camouflage outfit with the slip on elbow and knee pads used when making a jump. The helmet has a camouflage cover with netting over that to allow natural camouflage to be added. Rather than the standard brown combat boots worn by the armed forces, this Carabinieri wears highly polished black boots. In a webbed holster he carries a Beretta 9 mm. Corto (.380 ACP) automatic pistol. Over his shoulder is slung the folding stock BM59 'Paracadutisti' assault rifle.

34. NATO/West Germany: West German Airborne Feldwebel – Current.

This 1st Airborne Division sergeant wears standard G.F.R. combat dress with 'para' helmet. Over the helmet is a camouflage cover and netting for additional natural camouflage. A red beret may also be worn by G.F.R. paratroopers. On this figure's arm are the colors of the German Federal Republic. The single chevron denoting his rank of Feldwebel (Technical Sergeant) is worn on his epaulettes which are edged with the green Waffenfarbe of the infantry (which includes airborne and Alpine troops). Above the pocket on his right breast is the senior army parachutist's badge, indicating he has made at least 25 jumps. On the pocket flap he also wears a British parachutist's badge indicating additional parachute training at the British jump school at Brize Norton.

This Fallschirmjäger's weapon is the Heckler & Koch G3A4 rifle with butt retracted. Chambered for the 7.62 mm. NATO round and offering a cyclic rate of 500–600 RPM, the G3A4 ranks with the FN LAR as one of the best airborne assault rifles in the world. German paras have always favored the trench or boot knife, and this Feldwebel is no exception. Tucked into his left boot he carries the Mk3 Stiffelmesser which is virtually identical to the Gerber

Mark 1 boot knife.

35. NATO/West Germany: GSG-9 Counterterrorist Commando – Current.

Grenzschützgruppe 9 was formed after the killing of Israeli athletes on German soil during the 1972 Munich Olympics drove home the point that the German Federal Republic needed a counterterrorist unit. Rather than using a military unit (at least partially to avoid the charge of creating a new SS), it was decided to train a special group within the Federal Border Patrol. As a result, GSG-9 was formed as a special police unit within the Border Patrol.

The GSG-9 training program lasts 22 weeks and stresses mental and physical ability. Recruits come from the police, and only one in five makes it through the tough selection and training process. Training stresses hand-to-hand combat (especially karate), weapons familiarity, marksmanship, communications, high speed driving, helicopter insertions, and other physical skills. The physical training is combined with intensive academic training as well, the psychology and history of terrorist and counterterrorist theory being stressed.

GSG-9's most widely heralded use to date came on 17 October 1977 when twenty-seven members of GSG-9 successfully stormed a hijacked airliner at Mogadishu, Somalia. However, GSG-9 has carried out other missions with such success that few outside the unit even know about them.

The figure illustrated wears army style battle dress with the trousers bloused into combat boots. Over his tunic is a ballistic vest to protect him from small arms fire. He wears the West German paratroop helmet. On his hip is the Heckler & Koch P7 9 mm. automatic pistol in an open combat holster. This holster is far more suited to GSG-9's needs than the flapped case holster commonly used by the German police. The P7 is one of the most revolutionary weapons designs in years having a squeeze cocker which renders it instantly ready to fire as soon as the weapon is grasped yet instantly safe as soon as it is released. It is a very fast, accurate, and compact combat auto well suited to GSG-9's needs. The H & K P9S double action 9 mm. pistol is also used by GSG-9. In addition to his pistol, this figure carries the Steyr SSG 7.62 mm. NATO sniper's rifle with Kahles 3 to 9 power telescopic sight. The SSG is a bolt action rifle which uses a 5 round detachable box magazine. GSG-9 sniper/countersniper teams either use this rifle or the Heckler & Koch G3 SG/1 sniper's rifle. The G3 SG/1 is normally equipped with the Zeiss Diavari ZA 1.5 to 6 power telescopic sight, but a Zeiss/Orion starlight scope is also available for night use. Though a selective fire autoloading rifle, the G3 SG/1 is capable of good accuracy. Both 5 and 20 round magazines are available for the G3. Members of GSG-9 also use the Heckler & Koch MP5 9 mm. SMG and the MP5 SD 1 silenced version of the ultra compact MP5K SMG. Although they used British 'flash bang' stun grenades furnished by the SAS at Mogadishu, the Germans now have their own DT11B1 assault grenade which is made of laminated paper with sheet metal ends and contains 7 ounces of TNT flakes, all this in a package under 5 inches in length.

36. NATO/West Germany: GSG-9 Commander, Colonel Ulrich Wegener – Current.

Ulrich Wegener, who has commanded GSG-9 since its formation in 1972, is the senior counterterrorist commander in the world. In addition to supervising the formation and training of his counterterrorist unit, Wegener has found time to take parachute training with the Israelis and to accompany them on the Entebbe raid, to train with the FBI, and to work closely with the heads of other European counterterrorist units such as the British SAS CRW Wing and the French National Gendarmie Action Group.

In this illustration, Wegener wears the same basic combat dress as his men and carries an H & K 9 mm. auto pistol on his hip. He wears Federal Border Police rank on his epaulettes and GSG-9 insignia and tab on his upper sleeve. His beret is dark green, the standard border police color.

37. NATO/Belgium: Belgian Private, 1st Parachute Battalion – Current.

Belgian special units are concentrated primarily within a para-commando regiment, consisting of two parachute and one commando battalions as well as attached support units. Both the 1st and 3d (Parachute) Battalions wear the red beret, while the 2nd (Commando) Battalion wears the green beret.

The beret badge for members of the 1st Battalion is virtually identical to the British SAS winged dagger and bears the 'Who Dares Wins' motto. This beret badge commemorates the battalion's descent from the World War II Belgian SAS Squadron. The camouflage smock over green trousers is also reminiscent of those worn by British paratroopers.

This private carries one of the finest airborne weapons in the world – the FN FAL folding stock 7.62 mm. NATO rifle. With an effective range of 600 meters and a practical full auto rate of fire over 100 RPM (from 20 round box magazines), the FN FAL gives its user a lot of firepower and the ability to engage the enemy at a reasonable distance. Since Fabrique Nationale Herstal is based in Belgium, the armed forces of that country have ready access to some of the highest quality small arms in the world, the FN FAL, Browning 9 mm. Hi-Power pistol, Mitraillette Vigneron M2 SMG, and FN MAG machine-gun being just a few of the most widely known products of the Belgian armaments industry.

38. NATO/Portugal: Portuguese Commando Corporal – Angola, 1974.

Although there are Marine Commandos within the Portuguese Navy, the corporal illustrated is from an Army Commando unit. The Army Commando units were formed primarily for use as elite infantry in Portugal's colonial wars and were used only rarely in the airborne role. The red beret is worn by Portuguese commandos, while airborne troops wear a green beret with Air Force badge. The camouflage pattern worn by this corporal was well suited to wars in Africa where most of Portugal's colonies were located and where her armed forces were most likely to see combat.

For enlisted personnel on foreign service the rank insignia was worn on black slides on the shoulder straps as illustrated on this figure. His two red chevrons with point up indicate that he is a corporal. A single red chevron point up designates a lance corporal, while a single red chevron point down designates a private 1st class. Sergeants wear gold chevrons – three point down for lance sergeants, three point up for sergeants, and four point up for staff sergeants.

On a sling, this Commando carries the M3 version of the German 7.62 mm. NATO MG42/59 machine-gun which has been produced on licence in Portugal. This is the same basic weapon which was introduced into service with the Wehrmacht in 1942. Ammunition belts for the 11.5 kg weapon are carried wrapped around the corporal's torso.

39. NATO/Greece: Greek Paratrooper – 1975.

This paratrooper, as a member of an elite unit, is probably a professional soldier rather than a conscript. Rank badges are normally worn on the upper arm and differ for professionals and conscripts. A professional sergeant, for example, would wear three chevrons over a gold bar, while a conscript sergeant would wear only three chevrons. The camouflage battle dress is the normal uniform for the Greek airborne forces as is the green beret. The patch and tab are those of the Greek Parachute Regiment. On his left breast, this figure wears the free faller badge which may indicate that he is assigned to the special raiding battalion of the regiment.

He is armed with the U.S. M3 .45 ACP submachine-gun, usually known as the 'Grease gun'. Although this weapon dates from World War II, its knockdown power and reasonably low cyclic rate, 450 RPM, still make the M3 a devastating 'alley cleaner'.

40. NATO/Canada: Canadian Airborne Staff Sergeant – 1978.

The Canadian Airborne Regiment traces its roots to the 1st

Canadian Parachute Battalion which was formed at Camp Shilo, Manitoba, in 1942 and to the joint U.S./Canadian 1st Special Service Force, the 'Devil's Brigade' of World War II fame. (The Canadian element originally formed the 2nd Canadian Parachute Battalion.) In the post war years, Canada maintained small airborne components in her armed forces, perhaps the most famous of which was the Mobile Striking Force, which was, in effect, a group of airborne Arctic commandos. In 1968 the Canadian Airborne Regiment was formed at Edmonton where it remained until 1977 when it became part of the Special Service Force and was relocated at Petawawa, Ontario. Within the Regiment, the 1st Airborne Commando is French speaking, the 2nd Airborne Commando is English speaking, and the 3rd Airborne Commando is bilingual. Each of these Commandos is roughly of company strength. There are also parachute engineer, medical, signals, artillery, armored recce, and support units assigned to the Regiment. Heavy emphasis continues to be placed on operations in the Far North. Although about 800 candidates attend the basic parachute course each year, only 30 paratroopers, each of whom has already made 25 static line jumps, are selected each year for training as free fallers. Many of these free fallers end up in the pathfinder platoon or in the Sky Hawks, the 15 member parachute exhibition team.

The figure illustrated is a staff sergeant as is apparent from his three chevrons with crown. A sergeant wears three chevrons, a corporal two chevrons, and a lance corporal one chevron. On his U.S. style helmet he wears a U.S. camouflage cover, but his camo smock is of British pattern. His trousers are tucked into U.S. style jump boots. Reflecting the orientation towards the Far North of Canadian paratroopers are his snowshoes and insulated sleeping bag which, along with a rucksack, is below his reserve chute. Paras assigned to the Airborne Regiment wear wings with a white maple leaf, while parachute qualified personnel assigned to other units wear wings with a red maple leaf. Members of the Special Service Force can also be identified by their winged sword patch bearing the motto 'OSONS' which translates as 'We Dare'. In non-combat dress a maroon beret is worn.

The stock of this para's rifle is visible behind his snowshoes. The C1 assault rifle (the Canadian version of the L1A1) and the Sterling C4 SMG are both used by Canadian paratroopers. This figure, however, appears to be armed with a U.S. M-16.

41. NATO/Holland: Dutch Marine Sergeant – Current.

Along with the 'Korps Commandotroepen' of the Dutch Army, the Royal Dutch Marines are that country's principal elite force. The 1st Amphibious Combat Group consisting of about 600 men is based in Holland, while the 2nd Amphibious Combat Group also with a strength of about 600 men is based in the Netherlands Antilles. Stationed at the Van Braam Houckgeest Barracks in Doorn is the special counterterrorist unit of the Dutch Marines best known for its actions against South Moluccan terrorists. About 85 per cent of the Dutch Marines are professionals, while the remainder are national servicemen. Within the ranks of the Marines are combat swimmers (who wear a badge having red SCUBA tank and fins on a black background or gold dolphins on a black background), snipers (a red star on black background), paratroopers (winged parachute badge similar to that worn by the British), and specialists in winter warfare (white stag on a black and white shield).

The figure illustrated wears a heavy 'Commando' sweater with elbow and shoulder pads. His olive trousers have large cargo pockets. He wears the black beret of the Marines with gold anchor badge on a red background. Army Commandos wear green berets with a crossed Fairbairn-Sykes dagger badge. His rank is worn on his shoulder straps. Three gold chevrons indicate he is a sergeant of Marines. A sergeant major wears four gold chevrons, a corporal two yellow chevrons, a Marine 1st Class two red chevrons, and a Marine 2nd Class one red chevron.

This sergeant is travelling light with only a canteen and magazine pouch on his belt. His weapon is the Israeli Uzi which is a popular close combat weapon with the Dutch Marines.

42. NATO/Turkey: Turkish Paratroop Sergeant – 1970.

This sergeant is part of the Turkish Parachute Brigade. Many members of the Brigade made a combat jump in July 1974 on Cyprus.

He wears green Turkish battledress, though his jacket, at least, bears some resemblance to U.S. uniforms of the Korean War era. His helmet is very similar to the style worn by German paratroopers. On his left breast are his parachutist's wings. His weapon is the M1A1 Thompson SMG. Though at almost 5 kg, it is heavy for an airborne weapon by current standards, the .45 ACP 'Tommy Chopper' is still highly thought of by many. Its 700 RPM cyclic rate makes it hard to control in full auto fire, but with a 20 or 30 round magazine in place, the M1A1 can still throw a lot of 230 grain bullets rapidly. The H & K G3 rifle is also used by Turkish special troops.

43. Warsaw Pact/Soviet Union: Soviet Airborne Private – Current.

The Soviet airborne forces have a long history dating back to the 1930s when Red Army parachutists pioneered military parachuting, and some form of jump coverall and cloth or leather helmet similar to the ones worn by this private have been used throughout the existence of the Soviet airborne forces. Currently, the Soviets muster up to eight airborne divisions in the Vozdushno Desantnye Vojska (Independent Airborne Force) which are the elite of the Red Army ground forces. Spearheading the 1968 move into Czechoslovakia and the 1980 invasion of Afghanistan, the airborne forces act as the rapidly deployable reserve of the Soviet High Command. In a land war in Europe, Soviet airborne forces would, no doubt, be among the first enemy troops encountered by NATO fighting men. Soviet airborne forces are normally assigned one or more of the following missions: facilitate a breakthrough, delay enemy reserves, help envelop enemy troops, seize commanding heights, seize enemy anti-tank weapons, artillery, and atomic delivery systems, disrupt the enemy rear by destroying fuel and ammo dumps, seize airfields, bridges, or other objectives, and support river crossings or amphibious landings.

This paratrooper would jump and fight in his coverall and cloth helmet, no additional head protection being issued for combat. He is armed with the squad anti-tank weapon, the RPG-7 launcher. On his back he wears a pack for three extra HEAT rounds for his RPG-7.

44. Warsaw Pact/Soviet Union: Soviet Airborne Senior Sergeant – Current.

As befits his elite status, this Soviet paratrooper wears a distinctive uniform and carries a special weapon. His light blue beret, blue shoulder boards, and special arm badge as well as his striped t-shirt identify him as a member of the airborne forces. He also wears his parachutist's and Guards badges. The Soviet parachutist's badge, a richly enamelled white parachute on a blue background crowned by a red star, is one of the most attractive of all jump badges. The white gloves worn by this senior sergeant (his rank is indicated by the broad gold band on his shoulder boards) indicates that he is probably dressed for a parade, perhaps the traditional May Day flaunting of Soviet military might in which airborne troops frequently play an important role.

Of particular interest is this paratrooper's weapon, the new AKS-74. Built on the AKM-47 receiver but with an improved extractor, the AKS-74 is a lighter arm, much more suited to airborne use than the folding stock AKM. The AKS-74 uses a high-velocity 5.45 mm. round, but because of its muzzle brake, barrel climb is easily controllable even in full auto fire. Recoil is also reduced. To keep weight down and ease fabrication the AKS-74 utilizes a plastic magazine.

45. Warsaw Pact/Soviet Union: Soviet Airborne Sniper – Current.

This paratrooper is armed with the Dragunov (SVD) 7.62 mm. semi-automatic sniper's rifle. The weapon is fitted with a 4 power PSU-1 telescopic sight having an integral rangefinder, a battery-powered reticle illumination system, and infra-red night capability. This sophisticated sighting system gives the SVD an effective range out to over 1,000 meters in skilled hands, and its magazine capacity of 10 rounds and semi-auto mechanism grant it more firepower than bolt action sniper's rifles.

This paratrooper's camouflage clothing and the fact that he is a sniper are indicative that he is one of the special 'desant' troops trained for missions behind enemy lines. In the event of war, his target might well be a high-ranking NATO officer. Other members of these special units would sabotage NATO's nuclear stockpiles or carry out other pre-emptive acts to disrupt mobilization. Trained for both airmobile and HALO insertions, the special raiding units of the Soviet airborne forces (the Parashutno-Desantny Polk) are specialists in surprise attacks on the enemy's rear.

46. Warsaw Pact/Soviet Union: Soviet Airborne Sub-Lieutenant – Current.

Although normally viewed as a potential aggressor in the West, the Soviet Union's vastness coupled with potential enemies on its or its satellites' borders necessitates careful planning for the defense of the Motherland. Historically, the key to defending the Soviet Union has been the ability to fight in the bone-chilling cold and impassable snows of the Russian winter. Realizing the importance of equipping and training its elite troops for combat in harsh winter conditions, the Soviet Union has placed special emphasis on preparing the airborne troops to jump and fight under severe conditions.

Prepared for a cold weather jump, this officer wears a winter uniform consisting of a heavy fur collared coat, fur cap, gloves, and heavy trousers. White snow camouflage uniforms are also available for winter use, and a portion of the airborne forces are trained for ski operations. This sub-lieutenant wears both a main and a reserve chute, the main chute being deployed by a static line. Ripcords are, however, attached to both main and reserve chutes as well. When Soviet paratroopers first started using reserve chutes in the late 1930s, they followed the odd practice of opening both chutes when jumping. Now, however, though both chutes are worn, the reserve is only deployed in an emergency.

47. Warsaw Pact/Soviet Union: Soviet Naval Infantry Major – Current.

This major wears the service or field dress of the Naval Infantry. The officer's uniform differs from the enlisted man's by the addition of a black Sam Browne belt and a different beret badge. All ranks wear the blue and white striped t-shirt, black beret, and gold anchor sleeve insignia. A small fouled anchor emblem on the left side of the beret is also standard for all ranks. At least some Naval Infantry units have Guards status and will wear the Guard's badge over their right tunic pockets. The major's map case is as much a sign of rank as the star and red bars on his epaulets since in the Soviet armed forces only officers are normally authorized to make use of maps. In special units like the Naval Infantry, however, lower ranks may be privy to at least some operational plans.

As a Naval Infantry major, this officer possibly commands an entire Naval infantry brigade comprised of 3 amphibious motor rifle battalions, a battalion of PT76 light amphibious tanks, an AA battalion of self-propelled ZSU-23-4s, a company of M8 Gecko AA rocket launchers, an engineering company, and a communications company.

48. Warsaw Pact/Soviet Union: Soviet Naval Infantry Senior Lieutenant – Current.

This Soviet lieutenant is the commander of an amphibious motorized rifle company. Three of these companies are in each Naval Infantry battalion, with three such battalions making up a brigade. Currently, the Soviets deploy approximately 17,500 Naval Infantrymen in five brigades. The Baltic, North Sea, and Black Sea Fleets each have one Naval Infantry Brigade assigned, while the Pacific Fleet has two brigades assigned. (Note: Some authorities designate these units as regiments rather than bri-

gades, but because of their ability to operate as completely independent combat units, the author has chosen to use the brigade
designation.)

This officer wears a dark winter coat with black fur collar,
though white snow camouflage is also available for Arctic landings. Naval Infantrymen will also be seen wearing brown and
green camouflage with a matching helmet cover. Boots are calf
length black leather. The buckle on the black leather belt carries
the insignia of the Northern, Baltic, Black Sea, or Pacific Fleet to
designate where the Naval Infantryman's unit is assigned. His
weapon is the folding stock AKM-47, though it is likely the Naval
Infantry will soon be armed with the AKS-74. Spare magazines
are carried in the pouch on the right hip. The three stars on his
shoulder boards identify this officer as a senior lieutenant.
Within the Soviet rank system, there are three classes of lieutenant. In addition to the senior lieutenant, there are also a lieutenant, identified by two stars, and a junior lieutenant, identified by
one star.

49. Warsaw Pact/Soviet Union: Soviet Naval Infantry Commando – Current.

This Soviet frogman is from one of the four Naval Infantry
Commando platoons, one of which is assigned to each of the four
fleets. He is trained in SCUBA techniques and is also a qualified
paratrooper. The Naval Infantry Commando is skilled at infiltrating enemy beaches through HALO, submarine, helicopter, small
boat, or swimming insertions. His missions are very similar to
those of the U.S. SEALs or UDTs and British SBS combat swimmers. His likely targets would include enemy coastal installations
or enemy ships to which he would attach limpet mines. Dressed in
wetsuit and SCUBA gear, this frogman carries his diving knife
strapped to his calf. Other Soviet frogmen are assigned to army
units and may be used in river crossings or in sabotaging enemy
bridges.

50. Warsaw Pact/Poland: Polish Airborne 2nd Lieutenant – Current.

This officer is from the 6th Pomorska Airborne Division. Dressed for combat, he wears the Polish paratroop helmet rather than his red beret. Some type of flora has been tucked into the band around the helmet for camouflage. His battledress is relatively loose fitting and has numerous pockets making it well suited for use by parachute troops who never have enough pockets for the extra rations or ammo they like to jump with. His brown jump boots have buckles above the ankles, probably to give added support when landing on hard ground. On his right breast, this officer wears the Polish eagle and wreath parachutist's badge.

In his hand he carries the 9 mm. × 18 Makarov P-64 pistol. This double action semi-auto has a 6 round magazine capacity and is of Polish design. The weapon is issued with a spare magazine and the flap holster worn on this officer's hip. In this lieutenant's left hand is an offensive hand grenade which relies on concussion rather than fragmentation for its effect. This allows the grenade to be thrown while advancing without the necessity for taking cover, thus making it especially useful for airborne troops attacking static positions. Fuse delay on this grenade is about 4.5 seconds.

51. Warsaw Pact/Poland: Polish Naval Infantry Battalion Sergeant Major – Current.

The Polish Naval Infantry is a highly trained elite amphibious assault force equipped with the amphibious OT-62C APC. A dark blue beret with a badge consisting of a yellow anchor on a silver eagle is worn. The gray/black needle camouflage battle dress popular within the Warsaw Pact is worn with black boots and a white t-shirt with a blue stripe showing at the neck. The battledress is actually darker than that usually encountered with infantry units, black rather than gray being the dominant color. Rank designations are the same for the Naval Infantry as for Army units, two chevrons designating this NCO as a battalion sergeant major. As with the Soviet Naval Infantry, a black leather belt with a buckle bearing naval insignia is worn. The knapsack is also fairly typical of Warsaw Pact forces.

Although sometimes overshadowed by Czechoslovakia's famed armaments industry, Poland also has its own arms factories, and this Naval Infantryman carries the best known domestically produced weapon – the 9 mm. PM-63 Machine Pistol. This compact weapon fires the 9 mm. × 18 Makarov round at a cyclic rate of 650 RPM (practical rate is 75–100 RPM). 15, 25, and 40 round magazines are available. At a weight of 1.8 kg fully loaded with 25 rounds and an overall length of 33.3 cm, the PM-63 is quite compact. One interesting feature of this weapon is that no selector switch is incorporated. Instead, trigger pressure determines whether the weapon is fired in semi-auto or full-auto mode. There is also a compensator above the muzzle to keep climb down in full auto fire. Like the Israeli Uzi and the U.S. Ingram M-10, the PM-63s magazine fits into the grip, allowing sure changes under adverse conditions based on the 'hand finds hand' system. The PM-63s value to Naval Infantry forces lies strictly in its compactness and firepower, it being primarily a short range weapon.

52. Warsaw Pact/Czechoslovakia: Czech Paratroop Lance Corporal – Current.

This paratrooper is probably assigned to the Czech Airborne Brigade; however, other small special airborne commando and airborne recon units are also maintained in the Czech armed forces. The 7th Airborne Battalion at Holleschau, for example, is trained for special missions. The Czechs have an airborne tradition dating back to World War II, and their paratroopers have a reputation for being tough, well-trained, and competent.

Lance corporal's rank for this figure is designated by the single button on the right breast. A full corporal wears two buttons, one above the other, while combinations of buttons and stars indicate higher ranks. Actually, this system of indicating rank seems to be a relatively good one in combat, being readily visible to 'friendlies' (who already know what their NCOs and junior officers look like anyway) but not so visible to enemy snipers intent on picking off a unit's leaders.

In addition to the heavy duty plastic jump helmet which is worn, this trooper also has his red beret tucked into his belt. An identifying arrowhead shaped brown arm patch with subdued gold markings and a circle divided into red, white, and blue segments will sometimes be worn by Czech paratroopers as well. Combat boots are archaic appearing jump boots with buckles at the ankles. His bed roll and pack are on his back.

This lance corporal carries his squad's automatic weapon, the Vz59 GPMG in the bipod mounted LMG version. This easily portable and reliable machine-gun normally uses a 50 round box, but a 250 round box is also available. A 4 power telescopic sight or the PPN-2 infrared night sight can be fitted to the Vz59, and either of these could be advantageous for use in ambushes or raids behind enemy lines.

As a result of the well-established and widely respected Czech armaments industry, weapons like the Vz59 are designed and produced domestically, giving the Czechs more autonomy and higher quality in small arms than the other Warsaw Pact satellites. Czech arms merchants also have a reputation for being quite capitalistic in their sales approach, valuing hard currencies more than political ideology (i.e. it is hard to find someone Omnipol, the state arms producers, will not sell to).

53. Warsaw Pact/Bulgaria: Bulgarian Paratroop Corporal – Current.

The camouflage pattern worn by this corporal of the Bulgarian Parachute Battalion is issued to airborne units and to border guards. The ribbed leather helmet is worn by airborne troops, and a similar one is worn by motorized rifle units. Badges of rank are worn on the shoulder straps and are similar in pattern to those of the Soviet Union. Two parallel red bars indicate this para-trooper is a corporal. A lance corporal would have a single bar, while a sergeant (CSM) would wear three bars. The black combat boots appear more western in style than those used by other

Warsaw Pact countries. Magazine pouches, a knife bayonet, and a knapsack complete his basic equipment. He is armed with the AKMS assault rifle.

54. Warsaw Pact/East Germany: East German Airborne Regimental Lance Corporal – Current.

Much of the GDR's airborne potential rests with two para-commando units, the 40th and 5th 'Willi Sanger' Commando Battalions, which are held ready to undertake special missions behind NATO lines in case of war. East German paratroopers have also been turning up in the Middle East (Syria) and Africa (Angola) where they act as advisors to pro-Soviet airborne forces.

This paratrooper wears stone gray dress tunic and trousers with highly polished black jackboots and black leather belt. Only paratroopers wear the magenta beret, but the beret badge is the standard GDR cockade. On his right breast he wears his parachutist's badge. The orange collar tabs with white parachute are also unique to the airborne forces. On his left arm is a chevron identifying this paratrooper as a long service professional rather than a conscript. Regimental lance corporal's (Stabsgefreiter's) rank is indicated by the two bars on his shoulder straps.

55. Warsaw Pact/Hungary: Hungarian Paratrooper – 1980.

This Hungarian paratrooper wears a most practical jump jacket and trousers with padded elbows and knees. A camouflage cover and knapsack are carried, and he wears thick-soled paratrooper's boots. A camouflage beret is often worn in lieu of the helmet. On this beret is affixed a winged parachute badge-in gold for officers, in silver for NCOs, and in brown for other ranks. All three badges are made of cloth.

This para's weapon is the AMD submachine-gun, a Hungarian design based on the AKM, but having a shorter barrel (31.8 cm), a large muzzle brake, and a pistol grip. The AMD is chambered for the 7.62 mm. × 39 cartridge, the same as the standard AKM.

56. Warsaw Pact/Rumania: Rumanian Paratroop Corporal – 1979.

This trooper is a member of Rumania's 161st Parachute Regiment. He wears a useful parachutist's coverall of Soviet pattern with his parachutist's badge pinned to his right breast. His blue collar patches also mark him as a member of the Parachute Regiment. Corporal's rank is indicated by the wide stripes with blue regimental piping. A single stripe would mark him as a lance corporal. His parachutist's helmet is one of the more practical in use by any airborne unit, being a very sturdy 'crash helmet' design. The goggles are also a useful addition when jumping, especially since Rumanian paras use the BG-7M parachute, initiated by a static line (normally jumps are from 1,000 meters) which deploys a 3 foot stabilizer chute. At 500 meters, the jumper pulls a ripcord to deploy the main chute; however, as a safety device a barometric altimeter automatically deploys the main chute at 500 meters if the ripcord is not pulled. Rumanian paras also jump with a small inflatable rubber boat under their main chute pack. If the paratrooper lands in water he can use this self-inflating boat. This figure is lightly equipped with magazine pouches and knapsack. His weapon is the folding stock AKMS.

57. Non-Aligned/Yugoslavia: Yugoslavian Mountain Trooper – 1981.

This ski trooper is from one of Yugoslavia's mountain brigades, and in addition to being a skilled climber and skier, he is also trained in guerrilla warfare. All Yugoslav soldiers are, in fact, trained to operate as partisans if necessary, but the mountain troops, particularly, carry on the traditions of the World War II partisans who struck from, and retreated back into, the mountains. In many ways, Yugoslavian mountain troops receive training similar to that of U.S. Rangers.

This trooper is dressed for winter operations and wears his white snow camouflage outfit and his skis. During non-snow months, the mountain troops wear knee breeches, gray socks, and mountaineering boots. His weapon is the folding stock M64B

(70A), a Yugoslavian produced variation of the AK. One notable difference from the AK is that the M64B has a permanently attached spigot type grenade launcher.

58. Non-Aligned/France: French Colonial Paratrooper – Indochina, 1953.

This Colonial para might well have been a member of one of the three Colonial battalions which made the initial drop on 20 November, 1953, at Dien Bien Phu, thus opening the decisive battle of the French war in Indochina. If so, he would have been part of the largest of the 156 airborne operations mounted by the French in Southeast Asia. Throughout the French involvement, the Colonial, Metropolitan, and Foreign Legion paras – eventually totalling 25,000 airborne troops – fought courageously, but the lack of support, transport aircraft (C-47s were used), and supplies and equipment put them at a terrible disadvantage in conducting a widespread guerrilla war. As it turned out, the manpower for the 'oil slick' campaign the French foresaw just was not available.

This para wears camouflage of British pattern, while his helmet, boots, and webbed belt are of U.S. origin. Tucked into his helmet band is a field dressing. Though U.S. combat boots were standard issue to the paras, some substituted more practical canvas jungle boots. Of French origin are his canteen and ruck-sack. Like much of this para's equipment, his weapon, the M1A1 folding stock .30 Carbine, is of U.S. World War II vintage. The 15 round magazine was chosen over the 30 round curved magazine, since it was far less likely to catch in vines or brush while moving through the jungle. 30 round magazines have also had a tendency in some cases to cause jams. Overall performance of the M1A1 was disappointing, the .30 Carbine round lacking shocking power. However, the lightness of the weapon and of its ammunition made it a popular choice for airborne troops, and these considerations would have been especially critical for French paras in Indochina since they lacked transport aircraft and had to jump as light as possible.

59. Non-Aligned/France: French Paratroop Lieutenant Colonel Marcel Bigeard – Indochina, 1954.

Bigeard was the archetypal French para. In fact, Larteguey is believed to have based the main character in *The Centurions* on Bigeard. Enlisting in the Corps France (a Commando unit of sorts) in 1939, Bigeard later parachuted into France in 1944 to head the maquis of the Ariège. After rising through the ranks, he was commissioned as an officer and served in Indochina from 1947 to 1954, eventually commanding the 6th Colonial Paras and jumping with them into Dien Bien Phu. Sometimes known as 'Bruno', his *nom de guerre* in the Resistance, Bigeard raised morale upon his arrival at Dien Bien Phu just by his presence. Though imprisoned by the Vietnamese after the fall of Dien Bien Phu, Bigeard was released and fought in the counterguerrilla operations in Algeria as well.

Like such other great combat leaders as Nelson and Patton, Bigeard liked to wear his decorations, feeling they inspired confidence in his men and moved them to acts of courage. In this illustration he wears, among others, his Legion of Honor (Commander), British DSO, World War II Croix de Guerre, and TOE Croix de Guerre. Perched upon his head at a jaunty angle is his maroon para's beret with airborne badge, and on his right breast are his parachutist's wings. He wears green battle dress with large cargo pockets at the hips and a webbed belt. On his left sleeve the diamond shaped patch is his unit insignia. No weapon is worn, since Bigeard did not normally carry weapons in combat once he reached battalion command level. Upon his shoulders, he wears the three silver and two gold bars of a Lieutenant Colonel, but he did not trade the four silver bars of a major for them until his promotion during the Battle of Dien Bien Phu.

60. Non-Aligned/France: French Foreign Legion Paratrooper, 1st REP – Algeria, 1960.

Before its disbandment after the 1961 'Putsch', the 1st REP was the most decorated unit in the Foreign Legion. Although there were a few parachute operations in Algeria, more frequently, the paras were used on helicopter assaults and as shock infantry who moved in to finish the terrorists once they were located by conventional units. The Legion paras were also used for urban security duties in Algiers, being especially effective and ruthless in cleaning up the Casbah in the fall of 1957.

The Legion para illustrated is equipped for the urban security role rather than service in the 'bled'. His battledress is the striped pattern identified with the paras, and the sight of which was an anathema to terrorists because of their well-founded fear of the paras. Trousers are bloused into brown French combat boots. The green beret with ties hanging loosely at the rear and para beret badge is worn. Parachutist's wings are on his right breast.

Travelling light while on urban security duty, only a fighting knife and spare magazine pouches are worn on the webbed belt. The weapon is the MAT49 9 mm. SMG. At just under 5 kg in weight and at about 56 cm in length with butt retracted, the MAT49 is a compact and reliable close quarters weapon well suited for dealing with urban terrorists. Magazine capacity is 32 rounds, and for ease in carrying or during parachute operations, the magazine housing rotates forward with the magazine inserted, placing the magazine parallel beneath the barrel. Note that the para illustrated carries his weapon in the slung ready position with magazine down. The magazine also acts as the foregrip for the non-shooting hand, allowing the weapon to be held down in full auto fire. A grip safety is the only one employed, granting the MAT49 the ability to be brought into action very quickly. Though not an ideal weapon on the open battlefield, it makes an excellent 'Casbah sweeper'.

61. Non-Aligned/France: French 11th Parachute Division Trooper – 1979.

Most of France's airborne capability is concentrated in the 16,587 men of the 11th Parachute Division. This division, composed of long service professionals who proudly carry on the French para tradition, is based at Tarbes, but sub units are on duty all over the world. Among the regiments comprising the 11th D.P. are the

14th RPCT (Command & Signals), 1st RHP (Armored Infantry), 35th RAP (Artillery), 17th RGAP (Engineers), 1st RPIMa (Airborne Commandos/Special Forces); First Parachute Brigade: 3rd RPIMa (roughly equivalent to the former Colonial Paratroops), 8th RPIMa, 9th RCP (Chasseurs); Second Brigade: 1st RCP, 2nd REP (Foreign Legion Paras), 6th RPIMa. The 5th RHC (twenty SA-341 helicopters, fifteen SA-330 helicopters, and nine ALOUETTE III helicopters) is also assigned to lend the 11th D.P. airmobility. Two regiments, the 2nd RPIMa and 13th RDP (also a para-commando unit), are independent of the 11th D.P. Fixed wing transport capability is provided by Transall aircraft, though lift capability is available for only a fraction of the division at one time. Along with the Foreign Legion and the 9th Marine Division, the 11th D.P. is one of France's principal intervention units. In 1977–8 the 11th was used in Mauretania against Polisario guerrillas; in 1978 in aid of Chad against Libya; and in 1978 in Zaire.

The figure illustrated is equipped for a combat jump. He wears standard French helmet without cover but with strap fastened. (A red beret is worn for dress or walking out.) The cargo pockets of his uniform trousers appear to be stuffed with extra rations, cigarettes, or ammo in experienced para fashion. His rucksack is worn below his reserve chute. At the left shoulder is worn an orange scarf as a recognition symbol or field sign. Tucked beneath his reserve chute is a 9 mm. MAT SMG which despite its long service is still widely used by French troops. Spare 32 round magazines are carried in the pouch on the right hip. It should be noted that the 5.56 mm. MAS 'Bullpup' assault rifle is becoming the standard weapon among French special units.

62. Non-Aligned/France: French Foreign Legion Paratroop Lieutenant – Kolwezi, Zaire, May, 1978.

The 2nd REP made its first combat jump since Dien Bien Phu at Kolwezi on 19 May 1978 when three companies jumped from 600 feet to liberate Europeans being held by Communist rebels. The Legionnaires' chutes not having caught up with them, they used Zairian T10s which caused some jerry-rigging since there were no harness attachments for French leg bags. Additional units jumped to reinforce the 1st, 2nd and 3rd Companies the next day. By 21 May the rebels were routed, 250 of them being KIA, while more than 2,500 whites had been rescued – all for a loss of only five Legionnaires KIA and 25 wounded.

The 2nd REP, though part of the 11th Parachute Division, is based at Calvi on the coast of Corsica. In addition to being trained parachutists, its 650 Legionnaire paras are also skilled mountain and ski troops.

Showing the Legion's sense of style even in combat, the figure illustrated wears a tightly fitting camouflage uniform with tapered legs tucked into combat boots. His helmet is covered and has black tape ringing it. Although most Legionnaires jumped in their helmets, many wore their green berets once on the ground at Kolwezi. Lieutenant's rank is indicated by the two gold bars on his shoulders. A 2nd Lieutenant wears one gold bar, a captain three, and a major four. At his shoulder he wears a black scarf which was a field sign for the Kolwezi jump. The 'K' tab on his rucksack is for identification. His handgun is the 9 mm. MAS Model 1950 pistol. This weapon and the PAP Mle FL (A military version of the 15 shot MAB15) are the standard French military sidearms. Spare magazine pouches and fighting knife are also worn on his webbed belt. He holds an excellent map of the area of operations provided by French Army advisors to Zaire. Although this officer carries a pistol, MAT 49 SMGs and F-1 sniper's rifles were the primary weapons used at Kolwezi. Some paras also carried the Strim 89 mm. anti-tank rocket launcher which was used to knock out two rebel armored cars attempting a counterattack.

63. Non-Aligned/France: French Naval Infantry Commando – Current.

The term 'Marine' is somewhat misleading when applied to French units, since the 9th Marine Division is not an amphibious assault unit but is actually the descendant of the Colonial Infantry

Regiments. The Naval Infantry (or 'Marine') Commandos, on the other hand, are highly trained amphibious assault troops, many of whom are also airborne and/or SCUBA trained.

The Commando illustrated wears a standard camo jacket but wears shorts and canvas patrol boots rather than trousers and combat boots, indicating he is probably serving in one of France's possessions or former colonies in the tropics.

Slung over his shoulder is the 5.56 mm. MAS assault rifle. This short (75.7 cm) light (3.38 kg) weapon is now widely used among elite troops such as the Naval Infantry, Foreign Legion, and Paratroops. Among its interesting features are optional right or left side ejection and three round burst mode as an alternative to single shot or full auto. With the MAS's high cyclic rate of 900–1000 RPM, the three shot burst mode should be a real boon in controlling the weapon. As in the British Individual Weapon, the MAS's 25 round magazine fits behind the trigger and pistol grip. On his belt, this figure wears the MAS bayonet.

64. Non-Aligned/Austria: Austrian 'Schlangenfresser' Corporal – 1978.

'Schlangenfresser' means snake-eater and is the name given to graduates of the Austrian Ranger School at Hainburg. In addition to parachute training and extensive Alpine training (including parachute jumps into the mountains), 'Schlangenfresser' training stresses hand-to-hand combat, survival, woodcraft, raiding, and patrolling. Although officer cadets and certain other special troops receive airborne training as well as the Rangers, the graduates of the 'Schlangenfresser' School are considered the elite of the Austrian Army.

This corporal is immediately recognizable as a Ranger by his dark green beret. His para-commando wings consisting of a white winged parachute with vertical gold sword on a red-white-red center-piece and this same badge on his beret are further marks of the Ranger. Also unique to the Rangers is the light green collar patch. The two stars on this patch indicate the rank of corporal

(Korporal). A senior private (Gefreiter) wears one star, and a junior sergeant (Zugsführer) wears three stars in a triangular pattern.

This Ranger is armed with the 9 mm. Steyr MPi 69 SMG. The MPi 69 has some interesting features, not the least of which is its cocking method. To cock the weapon the sling must be given a backward pull while it is held at right angles to the gun. In practice this system is not 'soldier proof' and could cause problems in combat. This weapon's selective fire system is based on a dual pressure trigger. A short squeeze gives single shots while a sharp pull gives full auto fire. This is actually a good system since it eliminates fumbling for a selector switch in a tight situation. Magazine capacity is 25 rounds, and cyclic rate is a controllable 400 RPM. Except for the cocking system, the MPi 69 is one of the better SMG's around.

Many Austrian Rangers, Alpine troops, etc. are also trained as snipers, and they use the excellent SSG 69 7.62 mm. NATO sniper's rifle. Austrian special troops are now also using the 5.56 mm. Steyr AUG (Armee-Universal-Gewehr) assault rifle which is a light (3.3 kg) weapon constructed primarily of plastics and light alloys.

65. Non-Aligned/Switzerland: Swiss Grenadier Parachutist – Current.

This paratrooper is assigned to the para-commando company of the Swiss Air Force which is the principal airborne unit within the Swiss armed forces. This trooper wears the distinctive Swiss camouflage pattern with trousers tucked into black leather gaiters. His boots are metal cleated, a real advantage in the mountainous terrain of Switzerland. He also wears the well-known large Swiss helmet with camouflage cover. His weapon is the SIG StGW57 7.62 mm. assault rifle which is of Swiss design. This Grenadier Parachutist holds his rifle like a marksman, which he no doubt is, marksmanship standards in the Swiss armed forces being among the highest in the world. So proud and confident are the Swiss of their marksmanship that a Swiss officer, when asked by a German general how Switzerland's citizen army would cope should a German army outnumbering them by three to one invade the country, supposedly answered, 'Each Swiss soldier would shoot three times!' This paratrooper also carries a SIG bayonet which can double as a fighting knife at his waist.

Like the rest of the Swiss Army, the Grenadier Parachutists are not trained to fight an offensive war, but should anyone attempt to invade their homeland, their skills will be put to excellent use in raids and sabotage missions against the enemy rear. The Swiss vow to blow up all the mountain passes and fight to the last man is not uttered lightly, and the Grenadier Parachutists are experts at demolitions. Like the Israelis, the Swiss take their reserve system very seriously. Any possible enemy should take it just as seriously.

66. Non-Aligned: Spanish Paratroop Private – 1977.

This private from the Spanish Parachute Brigade wears the mottled camouflage uniform issued to the paratroopers with his brigade insignia on the left sleeve. Paratroopers also wear an olive green walking out dress with parachutist's badge on the right breast. His black beret and highly polished black jump boots are further symbols of his elite status as a paratrooper.

His weapon is the 9 mm. Star Z45 SMG with stock extended. This weapon is very similar to the German MP40, but despite the age of the design it is still a good close combat weapon. Magazine capacity is 30 rounds and cyclic rate is 450 RPM. Spanish paras also use the CETME 7.62 mm. assault rifle.

Along with the Spanish Foreign Legion and Spanish Marines, the Parachute Brigade continues to protect Spanish interests overseas in such places as Spanish Morocco.

67. Non-Aligned/Australia: Australian SAS Trooper – Current.

The Australian Special Air Service Regiment was formed in 1957 as an independent company. Since its foundation, the Australian

SAS has seen action in, among other places, Brunei and Vietnam. Currently, members of the SAS Regiment perform all Special Forces tasks within the Australian armed forces, functioning as para-and amphibious commandos; combat swimmers; and HALO, desert, and mountain troops. Counterterrorist responsibility also rests with the SAS. This diversity of missions requires troops of the highest order. Fortunately, the caliber of Australian soldiers has always been high, and volunteers for the SAS are put through a tough selection and training program which eliminates all but the most qualified.

The SAS trooper illustrated is equipped for an amphibious raid. He wears Australian camouflage dress with parachutist's wings on the sleeve and jungle boots. His weapon is the L34A1 Sterling silenced SMG for quietly eliminating enemy sentries. The Mk 5(L34A1) is basically the 9 mm. Mk 4 Sterling with silencer attached. The Mk 5 is virtually inaudible at 30 meters but is intended primarily for use as a single shot. In an emergency, however, it can be fired full auto. Magazine capacity is 34 rounds. As an additional silent killer this trooper also carries the flat pommelled Australian version of the classic Fairbairn-Sykes Commando dagger, a weapon designed for the quick elimination of the enemy via a thrust to the carotid artery.

Though this trooper is not wearing his, the Australian SAS wear a sand colored beret similar to that of their British counterparts.

68. Non-Aligned/South Africa: South African Recon Commando – Current.

The Reconnaissance Commandos, also known as 'Recces', are the elite of South Africa's armed forces. All Recces are parachute trained in both free fall and static line techniques. Some are also skilled combat swimmers. Their primary missions are to operate behind enemy (i.e. SWAPO or other guerrilla forces, especially those based in Angola) lines and to undertake cross border raids. Their missions are quite similar to those undertaken by Rhodesia's Selous Scouts during that country's counterterrorist war. Recces are expert trackers and can survive well in the arid bush country common to Southern Africa. At the end of his 42 weeks training period – some of the toughest in the world – the Recce Commando is a formidable fighting man.

The Recce illustrated is ready for a cross border operation, possibly into Angola. The black camouflage paint on exposed flesh keeps the fact that he is white from being obvious except at close quarters, and he can deal quite quickly with any guerrilla at close quarters. Disguising his race is important, though, when operating in areas populated solely by blacks. His brown bush hat and uniform also blend well with the earth and brush of Southern Africa. He carries the 7.62 mm. FN MAG machine-gun on a sling. Though a heavy load to hump for long distances, the FN MAG gives a lot of firepower in the type of close quarters firefight the Recces might expect to be involved in. Around his torso this Recce carries disintegrating link belts for his FN. Normal armament for the Recces is an FN/FAL, often with folding stock, and a fighting knife such as the one illustrated. Some Recces choose custom fighting knives such as the excellent 'Warlock', a blackened stiletto designed with night raids in mind, made by famed South African knife maker Peter Bauchop.

69. Non-Aligned/Rhodesia: Rhodesian Selous Scout, 1978.
Perhaps the best comment on the fighting ability of the Selous Scouts is the fact that during Rhodesia's anti-terrorist war they accounted for more dead 'terrs' than the rest of the Rhodesian Army combined. Formed in 1974 as the Tracker Combat Unit and eventually performing long range recon missions, tracking terrorists internally, and undertaking cross border raids against terrorist strongholds, the Selous Scouts were highly skilled, parachute trained long range recon/raiders. Their selection process was somewhat similar to that of the British SAS. In addition to parachute training, bush survival and tracking were emphasized during Scout training. Clandestine and counterguerrilla skills were also taught. The Selous Scouts normally made operational jumps from about 500 feet using the T10 parachute, but many

members of the unit were also HALO specialists. Their primary transport aircraft was the venerable Dakota. For combat jumps, the Selous Scouts usually carried only ammo, medical supplies, water, and rations for two days plus their weapons. Their ruck-sacks were dropped later.

In August, 1976, the Selous Scouts launched the first cross border strike against terrorist bases in Mozambique. In that raid alone, they killed 1,184 terrorists. Later, the Selous Scouts under-took many missions in conjunction with the Rhodesian SAS which had a strength of 110 men, many of them former members of the British SAS. By comparision, the Selous Scouts numbered at the maximum about 700 men. Both of these units were especially feared and hated by the terrorists, perhaps the best comment on their combat effectiveness. As a result of this hatred, many former Selous Scouts and Rhodesian SAS troopers left Rhodesia after Mugabe came to power, probably a smart move since members of the SAS had at one time been sent to assassinate him. Now serving in the South African forces, many former Selous Scouts and Rhodesian SAS troopers continue their war against Communist backed terrorists.

The figure illustrated wears the standard Rhodesian camou-flage uniform with the distinctive Rhodesian camouflage hat with attached neck flap. His boots are also standard Rhodesian issue brown combat boots as is his webbed gear. It should be noted that members of the Selous Scouts had a lot of freedom in choice of uniforms and often wore shorts and a sleeveless t-shirt when operating in the bush. It was not entirely unheard of, either, for Scouts to turn up in the guise of East German advisors to Frelimo, Zipra, or Zanla. For dress wear the Selous Scouts wore a sand colored beret.

This Scout's primary weapon is the FN FAL 7.62 mm. NATO rifle but captured Soviet AKs were also frequently used. In his left hand he carries a loaded 20 round magazine. Often spare maga-zines would be carried in chest pouches of Rhodesian design. This Scout also carries a 9 mm. Beretta Model 92 double action auto-matic pistol in a U.S. military style shoulder rig, a possible indication that he is one of the 25 or so U.S. Vietnam veterans who served in the ranks of the Selous Scouts.

70. Non-Aligned/Israel: Israeli Paratroop Staff Sergeant – Current.

In 1954 Moshe Dayan combined Unit 101, which had been charged with reprisal raids, and the Israeli Independent Paratroop Battalion. The new unit was designated 202 and became the basis for many of the future successes of the Israeli paras. Members of Unit 202 became exceptionally skilled at night fighting, aggressively closing with the enemy and settling the issue with SMGs, grenades, and knives. The paratroopers were used as spearheaders and also as examples for the rest of the IDF.

Although Israeli paratroopers have made combat jumps, they are best known for their aggressive counterterrorist actions against the PLO and their use as shock troops during the 1967 War. In both the 1967 and 1973 Wars, Israeli paratroopers also carried out successful airmobile assaults on key enemy positions. Israeli paratroopers gained additional renown as the main striking force in the 3 July 1976 Entebbe Airport hostage rescue.

The paratrooper illustrated wears current Israeli battle dress and webbed gear. Instead of his helmet, he wears the red beret of the IDF airborne forces. The three bars with leaf on his sleeve indicate the rank of staff sergeant (Samal-Rishon). A lance-corporal (Turai-Rishon) wears one bar, a corporal (Rav-Turai) two bars, and a sergeant (Samal) three bars. His weapon is the Israeli produced Galil SAR assault rifle which has recently replaced the Uzi SMG, the standard arm of Israeli paras for 20 years. The SAR is the folding stock version of this weapon. With stock folded overall length is only 61.4 cm, 33 cm of which is barrel. The SAR weighs 3.65 kg. The weapon is selective fire, offering practical full auto capability of over 100 rpm. 12, 35, and 50 round magazines are available for the Galil. Although the Uzi remains an excellent close quarters weapon, the Galil grants the paras greater range, knockdown power, and penetration.

71. Non-Aligned/Israel: Israeli Paratroop Corporal – Current.

All Israeli paratroopers are volunteers who have completed up to a year and one-half of rigorous training. This training emphasizes practical skills such as weapons use, demolitions, clandestine cross border ops, and field medicine. Physical training is rough, and no matter what the weather Israeli paras live under canvas in the Judean Hills during the toughest part of their training. After completing jump school, many are chosen to specialize in HALO techniques which are sometimes used for clandestine insertions into 'Fatahland' (Southern Lebanon). Night operations are also stressed during Israeli airborne training as are helicopter assault tactics.

In raids against PLO camps in Lebanon or on other special missions, Israeli paras usually get an early baptism of fire, even in 'peacetime'. Members of special units like the GHQ unit and the 269 Counterterrorist Unit are normally drawn from the airborne forces.

This corporal who is probably assigned to one of the five parachute brigades has just completed a training jump and is removing his reserve chute. He wears standard Israeli battle dress bloused into brown combat boots. His helmet is the ballistic nylon one normally used by the paras but covered with a camo cover.

72. Non-Aligned/Israel: Israeli Para-Frogman – Current.

Israel's own long coastline and the lengthy coastlines of some of the Jewish State's principal enemies have made para-frogmen an important striking force within the IDF. Assigned to the Naval Infantry Commandos, these frogmen are trained as paratroopers and as combat swimmers. They are experts at demolitions, and most are HALO qualified. Used currently for hit-and-run missions against PLO bases along Lebanon's coast, Israeli frogmen previously operated against Egyptian ships and shore installations in the Gulf of Suez. Israeli frogmen are also used to check the keels of Israeli ships and for underwater patrols because of the danger posed by PLO frogmen.

This combat swimmer is lightly equipped. He wears his wetsuit and mask but not flippers or tanks. Strapped to his left leg is his underwater/fighting knife. His weapon which was probably carried in a waterproof container while swimming is the Uzi 9 mm. SMG. Though strictly a close quarters weapon, at 47 cm in length with stock retracted, the Uzi's compactness makes it a good choice for the frogmen. At 4.13 kg with a fully loaded 32 round magazine, it is reasonably heavy, though. Cyclic rate is 550–600 RPM, but practical full auto rate is only about 128 RPM (four magazines full, though like most pros the Israelis probably top off the first magazine after chambering a round). This frogman would not even achieve the practical rate since to save weight while swimming he carries only the magazine in the weapon and two spares in pouches on his hip. He is equipped for a raid rather than a firefight. Though the Israeli armaments industry has created some interesting special weapons, especially for clandestine use, to the best of the author's knowledge, no special weapon or special version of the Uzi has been developed especially for the frogmen.

73. Non-Aligned/Egypt: Egyptian Incursor Commando – Current.

Incursors from Egyptian commando battalions were the first troops across the Suez Canal during the 1973 Yom Kippur War against Israel, and they provided the spearhead for Egypt's early advances. Currently, Egypt maintains five Commando Groups as part of her Special Forces. Incursors are the Egyptian equivalent of the U.S. SEALs, being trained as combat swimmers as well as amphibious raiders.

This incursor carries an AKMS with stock folded and 30 round magazine in place. On his webbed belt he carries only spare magazines and grenades, the ability to travel light and fast necessitating the exclusion of extraneous equipment. A combination underwater/fighting knife, useful for underwater operations and also for silently eliminating sentries, is strapped to his left leg. His hooded wetsuit offers excellent night camouflage for small boat operations.

When in dress uniform, commandos can be identified by their

badge, a gold eagle with black feathers attacking a gold dragon with red scales.

74. Non-Aligned/Egypt: Egyptian Paratrooper – Current.
This paratrooper is assigned to one of Egypt's two parachute brigades. Trained for both airborne and airmobile assaults, Egyptian paras were used in helicopter operations during the 1973 war against Israel. At least some parachute units are also kept on alert for possible deployment against Libya.

Although this paratrooper wears the brown beret currently in use with the airborne forces, a red beret has also been worn. His camouflage pattern is a variation of the spotted tan 'leopard' pattern popular throughout the Middle East. Rather than brown spots, though, the camouflage worn by Egyptian paras during joint maneuvers with U.S. 101st Airborne troops from the RDF bore green spots on a dark tan background and closely resembled World War II German SS camouflage.

On a sling, this para carries the RPD 7.62 mm. × 39 mm. light machine-gun. This 9 kg (with fully loaded magazine) machine-gun has a cyclic rate of 650 RPM. Fired from the prone position with the RPD resting on its bipod, it is a reasonably accurate weapon out to ranges of 500 meters. The 100 round drum magazine contains two 50 round belts.

75. Non-Aligned/Oman: Sultan of Oman's Special Force Lieutenant – Current.
The British SAS has had official and unofficial involvement in Oman for some time, and the Sultan's Special Force shows a strong SAS influence. The unit was formed in 1977 from inhabitants of the Jebel area of Dhofar. Recruits were chosen from this area because of their reputation for military ability (many members of the Trucial Oman Scouts had come from Jebel) and for their loyalty to the crown.

The beret, lanyard, backing for the unit's shoulder title, and stable belt (when worn) of the Sultan's Special Force are royal purple. Originally orange was to be the beret color, but royal purple was chosen as a more suitable color. The beret badge is similar to the Special Air Service badge and bears the 'Who Dares Wins' motto in Arabic. Parachutist's wings are also of SAS pattern. The gray/green uniform and desert boots are very practical choices for use in the desert. Two stars on the shoulder straps identify this officer as a lieutenant. In his right hand he holds a British prismatic compass, an important instrument for navigation in the desert. In his left hand is the receiver of a British A41 radio. On his hip he wears a 9 mm. Browning Hi-power pistol with British 58 pattern webbed belt and holster. This holster has a built-in pocket for one spare magazine. The choice of the Browning 9 mm. may also have been influenced by the SAS, members of which armed with their ever-present Hi-Powers at one time acted as bodyguards for the Sultan of Oman.

76. Non-Aligned/Iraq: Iraqi Special Forces Trooper – Current.

The Special Forces Brigade of Iraq incorporates both airborne and commando troops. Originally the Iraqi Special Forces received training from the U.S. Special Forces, but more recently advisors will have been from the Soviet Union. This trooper's camouflage is well suited to the battlefields of the Middle East, combining the hues of sand, earth, and vegetation. His boots also seem designed for combat in a hot, dusty climate since the canvas upper portions allow good air circulation, while the soles give good traction even during amphibious operations. His weapon, reflecting the Soviet influence in Iraq, is the folding stock AKMS-47. One of the most ubiquitous of all current weapons, the AK-47 fires the 7.62 mm. × 39 mm. Soviet cartridge. The 'M' in the weapon's designation indicates the use of a stamped receiver for ease of manufacture, while the 'S' indicates the folding stock version of the weapon. Magazine capacity for the AKM is 30 rounds and cyclic rate is 600 RPM. Practical rate of fire is about 100 RPM. Despite its popularity in the Middle East, the AK's lack of long range killing power has sometimes proven a disadvantage in combat within the region's vast open spaces.

77. Non-Aligned/Iran: Iranian Special Forces Trooper – Current.

Indicating the close relations between the Iranian Special Forces and their U.S. counterparts before the fall of the Shah, this trooper still sports his green beret, U.S. style webbed pistol belt, and U.S. pattern combat boots. Camouflage is of the leopard spot variety popular in the Middle East where a tan colored background with brown splotches is effective camouflage. Former members of the German SS who advised many Middle Eastern armies in the post-war years may also have influenced this choice of pattern since some Middle Eastern camouflage patterns are direct descendants or outright copies of wartime SS patterns.

This trooper's weapon is the Heckler & Koch G3A4 retractable stock 7.62 mm. NATO assault rifle. Magazine capacity of the G3A4 is 20 rounds. Although this trooper looks a bit 'scruffy' by Western standards and by the standards of the Shah's armed forces, indications are that Iranian Special Forces and airborne troops have given a good account of themselves in the war against Iraq. Originally the Special Forces totalled a brigade, but purges of troops loyal to the Shah and the fighting against Iraq have, no doubt, inflicted casualties on the Special Forces.

78. Non-Aligned/Jordan: Jordanian Paratroop Lieutenant Colonel – 1967.

The distinctive parachutist's helmet, parachute unit insignia on his arm, and bloused trousers identify this officer as a member of the paratroopers. His rank is denoted by the crown over a single star on his epaulets. A full colonel would have a crown over two stars, a brigadier a crown over three stars. A major wears a single crown, a captain three stars, and 1st and 2nd lieutenants two and one stars respectively. This officer's sidearm is probably a Smith & Wesson revolver in .380/200 British caliber, though some .38 Special S & Ws are also used in Jordan. The weapon is worn in a British style webbed holster.

The Jordanian army has enjoyed the reputation of being one of the best in the Middle East for the last thirty years, partially, at least, due to the inherent fighting qualities of the Bedouins and partially due to training during the days of the Arab Legion by soldiers of fortune like Glubb Pasha and Peake Pasha. The Bedouins' native dash and flair for raiding should enable them to make excellent airborne soldiers.

Currently most of Jordan's airborne troops are concentrated in four Special Forces battalions which can be identified by their maroon berets.

79. Non-Aligned/India: Indian Paratrooper – 1973.

India's paratroopers have a long and proud tradition dating back to late 1941 when the 50th Indian Parachute Brigade was formed as part of the British Indian Army. From that time until the present, India has maintained a strong airborne tradition. Indian paras have seen service in Korea, along the Tibetan border, and against Pakistan in the 1965 and 1971 (Bangladesh) wars. Currently, two parachute brigades, the 50th and 51st, are maintained. On 11 December 1971 near Tangail the 2nd Parachute Battalion, 49th Parachute Field Battery, and medical and support troops made India's most recent combat jump during the drive on Dacca. As part of her parachute forces, India also maintains two para-commando battalions, the 9th and 10th, both of which saw action in the Bangladesh War.

Indicative of the origins of India's parachute forces are the British style camouflage smock and trousers worn by this figure. His maroon paratrooper's beret is also similar in style to that worn by the British Parachute Regiment. It bears the winged parachute badge of the Indian Parachute Regiment. The para-commando battalions wear a winged dagger badge similar to that of the SAS.

Although this figure wears his T10 parachute and T7 reserve chute, they appear to be for parade purposes since the harness straps which would normally pass beneath the crotch are not fastened. Also he carries his FN rifle slung rather than in the leg bag used for operational jumps.

For such jumps Indian paras deploy from the Soviet AN-12 transport which can carry 62 paratroopers. Normally on combat jumps rations and ammunition for 3–4 days are carried by each jumper.

80. Non-Aligned/India: Indian Paratroop Lieutenant Colonel – 1971.

This LTC would probably be the commanding officer of one of India's parachute battalions. The fact he wears a maroon pagris (turban) rather than a beret indicates that he is a Sikh, it having been established as far back as 1945 that Sikh paratroopers could wear their pagris in lieu of other headgear. A special padded protective helmet was even developed so that they could wear the pagris while jumping. He does, however, wear the unit beret badge. It should be noted that LTC is the highest rank which wears unit insignia on the headgear, colonels and above substituting rank insignia instead. On his right sleeve, this officer wears his parachutist's wings, while on his left sleeve he wears his formation sign, the Shatrujeet (a winged female centaur shooting a bow and arrow). On his left pocket he wears red jump indicator wings which show he has made at least 100 descents. Yellow would indicate 50 descents and blue 25 descents.

81. Non-Aligned/Thailand: Thai LRRP – Current.

Thai Special Forces, LRRPs (Tiger Scouts), and Rangers are all used along Thailand's borders against Communist guerrillas infiltrating from Laos. Members of Thai special units are parachute trained and most are graduates of the Ranger School (which awards a badge having a tiger clenching a sword between its teeth).

This Tiger Scout wears a locally produced camouflage pattern, one of the dozen or so in use with the Thai armed forces. As did many U.S. Special Forces troopers in Vietnam, Thai Rangers and Special Forces often favor all black uniforms rather than camouflage patterns. This trooper's weapon is the M-16, for which he wears a bandolier of extra magazines across his shoulder. To travel light, he uses the long range patrol pack, also of U.S. pattern. His boots are U.S. style jungle boots well suited for the parts of Thailand where he will operate.

82. Non-Aligned/People's Republic of China: Paratrooper – Current.

Currently, the People's Republic of China musters three parachute divisions based in Wuhan Military Region. These paratroopers are under air force control and serve as a strategic reserve. Lightly equipped, the Chinese parachute forces are best suited for raiding missions or jumps to seize key locations just ahead of advancing ground forces. Probably based on Soviet experiences with airborne troops in World War II and on the guerrilla heritage of the People's Liberation Army, assistance to guerrillas is also seen as a high priority airborne mission.

This paratrooper wears a one piece jump coverall similar to the type worn by Soviet airborne forces. The soft ribbed parachutist's helmet also bears a marked resemblance to those used by some Warsaw Pact countries. This figure's weapon is the Chinese Type 56 folding stock assault rifle, a copy of the AK-47. For raiding or assassination missions, Chinese paratroopers might also be equipped with the 7.65 mm. Type 64 silenced pistol or the 7.62 mm. Type 64 silenced SMG. In the figure's right hand is the new Type 79 mini-anti-tank rocket launcher, a compact, efficient weapon, well suited to the needs of the PLA's lightly equipped paratroopers.

83. Non-Aligned/Nationalist Chinese (Taiwanese): Amphibious Commando – 1960.

This predecessor to the current Long Range Amphibious Recon Commando is a member of only one of the many highly trained special units within the Taiwanese armed forces. In addition to amphibious commandos, highly competent paratroopers, Special Forces troops, and para-frogmen are maintained in a high state of combat readiness. Reportedly, a certain amount of exchange training has taken place between the special units of Taiwan, Israel, and South Africa, all three countries having formed a loose technical alliance based on their common isolation with numerically superior foes on their borders. In the case of Taiwan, only about 100 miles of ocean separates it from the People's Republic of China. The nearness of this mammoth enemy does not, however, seem to daunt Taiwanese special units. On the contrary, it has been the author's observation that the Taiwanese elite forces are entirely prepared for (and even anticipate undertaking) missions on the mainland and feel confident of successfully completing them.

Some of this confidence may stem from the fact that amphibious commandos such as the one illustrated have, in fact, been operating along the coasts of mainland China gathering intelligence for more than 20 years.

The figure illustrated is equipped for some type of beach incursion, being part of a unit making a clandestine insertion via rubber assault boat or IBS (Inflatable Boat, Small). He wears a camo head cloth and camo t-shirt with dark shorts. The black sneakers are well-suited to stealthy movement and sure footing when coming ashore through the surf. Exposed body parts are blackened for night ops. His firearm is the U.S. M2 Carbine, the selective fire version of the ubiquitous M1 Carbine. Because of their compact size and light weight, both of these carbines have enjoyed great popularity with U.S. allies in Asia. The U.S. Ka-Bar fighting knife and U.S. Mark 11A1 'Pineapple' grenade are also carried, the Ka-Bar, no doubt, being intended for the silent elimination of sentries, though Taiwanese special troops are also martial arts experts and could eliminate sentries bare handed if necessary.

84. Non-Aligned/Republic of Vietnam: Special Forces (LLDB) – 1970.

The LLDB (Luc Luong Duc Biet), the Vietnamese Special Forces, worked with the U.S. Special Forces on implementing the CIDG program, and LLDB units had U.S. Special Forces advisors. As with the U.S. Special Forces, the green beret is worn, the beret badge consisting of a winged parachute. Some LLDBs wore U.S. leaf or 'Tiger Stripe' camouflage, but this sergeant wears an indigenous pattern. Some locally produced 'jungle suits' even had two camouflage patterns on the same suit, the front being of leaf or brush pattern, while the rear was of dead leaf or ground cover pattern to increase concealability while lying prone. The parachutist's wings are worn on the left breast, and the ARVN Special Forces insignia is on the left sleeve. There are variations in this insignia, but all incorporate the leaping tiger (representing ferocity), the parachute (representing infiltration), and the three lightning bolts (representing air, sea, and land capability). The green shield is representative of the jungles and mountains where the LLDB operated. The insignia illustrated was adopted in 1963 and was standard from that point on. U.S. type webbed gear and combat boots are worn. The weapon is the CAR-15 version of the M-16 which has an overall length of only 71.1 cm with butt retracted as compared with 99 cm for a full sized M-16. The CAR-15 was quite popular with both U.S. and ARVN Special Forces both of whom found it more suitable for close quarters encounters with the enemy.

85. Non-Aligned/Indonesia: Indonesian Police Mobile Brigade Sergeant First Class – Current.
The Police Mobile Brigade is an elite airborne unit of the police which among other duties functions as the Indonesian counter-terrorist unit. The dark blue beret, red scarf, and insignia on the sleeve are special distinctions worn by the PMB. The uniform is the standard Mobile Brigade field uniform bloused into the combat boots. On this figure's left breast is the basic police parachutist's badge. The two gold chevrons indicate the rank of sergeant first class, the third highest NCO rank in the PMB. His weapon is the U.S. M-16 rifle.

86. Non-Aligned/Republic of Korea: Special Forces Trooper – Current.
The ROK Special Forces have a well deserved reputation for toughness. Even professionals like the U.S. Special Forces and Australian and New Zealand SAS who served with ROK 'Tigers'

in Vietnam were particularly impressed with them. In addition to being airborne qualified and highly trained in infantry skills, each ROK Special Forces trooper is a black belt in one of the martial arts, normally Taekwondo. Training is constant with up to $4\frac{1}{2}$ hours per day being spent practising hand-to-hand combat.

Realizing that war with North Korea is an ever present possibility, the ROK Special Forces engage in tough realistic training exercises to prepare themselves for missions in the North should war come. The Special Forces are also employed for dangerous missions along the DMZ such as clearing North Korean tunnels. ROK black berets have also been used as the pursuit units when North Korean raiders have infiltrated into the South. Their kill ratio on these missions is very high!

The trooper illustrated wears a spotted 'Tiger' camouflage suit which is similar to one worn by the U.S. Marines in World War II. Cammies are the standard uniform of the ROK Special Forces, and the reputation of the 'Tigers' is such that the sight of a camouflage uniform topped by a black beret even in Seoul's toughest areas is enough to cause troublemakers to hurriedly depart. Upon his left breast is the free faller's para badge with gold star indicating at least 100 jumps. The beret is black with the Special Forces badge. U.S. style combat boots are worn and the U.S. M-16 rifle is carried.

Distinctive pocket patches will sometimes be encountered for each ROK Special Forces Brigade. The Special Warfare patch bears a lion, the 3rd S.F. Brigade an eagle, the 5th S.F. Brigade a dragon, the 7th S.F. Brigade a Pegasus, the 9th S.F. Brigade a winged cat on a parachute, the 11th S.F. Brigade a bat over a lightning bolt, and the 13th S.F. Brigade a panther.

87. Non-Aligned/Vietnam: Vietnamese Parachute Nurse – Current.

Females are given parachute training in Communist Vietnam, and this nurse is a fully qualified paratrooper. She wears a Soviet style jump coverall and also has a Soviet style cloth or leather parachutist's helmet which is tucked into the large cargo pocket on her leg. Her canvas and rubber boots are well suited to wear in the jungle but do not give much ankle support should she wear them while jumping. Although her medical kit appears to be well stocked, medicines have been in short supply in Vietnam during the last few years.

88. Non-Aligned/Chile: Chilean Special Forces Trooper – Current.

This member of the Chilean Special Forces has been trained as both a parachutist and a commando at the School of Parachutists and Special Forces at Peldehue. The Chilean Special Forces maintain close ties with the U.S. 7th Special Forces Group in Panama, and many Chilean para-commandos receive additional training with their U.S. counterparts.

Three points set this figure apart and identify him as a member of the Special Forces. Most obvious is his black beret which is worn only by the Special Forces. On the beret he wears the Special Forces beret badge consisting of a parachute behind crossed jungle knives. A condor's wings surround the badge and claws grasp the knives. Finally, he wears a senior parachutist's badge on his left breast.

A Special Forces patch will sometimes be encountered in wear. It consists of an oval bearing a black condor and parachute with a gold dagger on blue background. At the top are the words 'Escuadron Fuerzas Especiales' and at the bottom 'Division De Caballeria'. A pathfinder patch bearing a gold torch and arrows and the word 'GUIAS' on a blue felt background and a jumpmaster patch bearing a white parachute and hand with downward pointing finger on a blue background may also be seen, especially around the para/commando school.

His weapon is the Ingram M-10 SMG. This weapon which is available in both 9 mm. and .45 ACP calibers bears some similarities to the Israeli Uzi, but at 26.9 cm in overall length with stock retracted and 3.82 kg in weight with a fully loaded 30 round magazine in place, it is much more compact. Practical rate of full auto fire is about 90 RPM (96 if 32 round mags are used), though cyclic rate is a difficult to control 1,000 + RPM.

89. Non-Aligned/Japan: Japanese Paratroop PFC – Current.

This member of Japan's Parachute Brigade helps carry on the combat traditions established by the highly competent Japanese Army and Special Naval Landing Force paras who jumped to seize key installations in the Dutch East Indies during World War II.

This paratrooper is dressed for a parade and wears the brightly individualistic Japanese camouflage uniform. The white scarf, black gloves, highly polished U.S. style combat boots, and polished helmet with parachute brigade insignia all contribute to this figure's smart appearance. On his sleeve he wears the patch of the 1st Airborne Brigade, and on his left breast are his parachutist's wings. A cloth freefaller's badge bearing a white winged parachute with a yellow disk containing the letters 'FF' is also worn by qualified Japanese jumpers. Below his brigade patch are the two chevrons of a private 1st class. One chevron is worn by a private and three by a leading private.

This figure's weapon is the Japanese Type 64 rifle which is produced by Howa Machinery Company, Ltd. This weapon is chambered for a reduced charge version of the 7.62 mm. NATO round to allow for the smaller size of Japanese soldiers. The Type 64 uses 20 round magazines and fires at the low cyclic rate of 470 RPM. For parade purposes, his bayonet is fixed.

90. Non-Aligned/Panama: Panamanian National Guard Paratrooper – 1972.

This Guardsman's uniform reflects the close ties between the U.S. and Panama. His fatigues bear a resemblance to U.S. 'greenies', and his combat boots are of U.S. style. Webbed gear is also of U.S. pattern. His red beret and parachutist's badge on the left breast help distinguish this trooper as one of the elite among the National Guard. His weapon is the obsolescent but still ubiquitous M1A1 folding stock .30 Carbine. Because of the heavy jungles in parts of Panama, the machete in his right hand is a very useful implement which can double as an effective weapon in the hands of skilled wielder. Panamanian paratroopers maintain close contact with the U.S. 7th Special Forces which are stationed in Panama and as a result the Panamanian paras are relatively well-trained and competent by Central American standards.

91. Non-Aligned/Brazil: Brazilian Paratrooper – 1972.

This paratrooper wears typical Brazilian camouflage battledress bloused into high brown combat boots. Olive green uniforms similar to those of the U.S. Army in the late 1960s and early 1970s were also worn by the Brazilians. This paratrooper is chuted up for a jump but is lightly equipped. His weapon is the Beretta Model 12 9 mm. SMG which is an excellent close quarters weapon being readily controllable because of its reasonably low cyclic rate of 550 RPM. 20, 30, and 40 round magazines are available for the Model 12. Brazilian paratroopers have also been equipped with a locally produced version of the Danish Madsen SMG known as the INA 953. This weapon is chambered for the .45 ACP round. This trooper's yellow shoelaces seem to indicate some type of unit honor since only paratroopers appear to wear them.

92. Non-Aligned/Brazil: Brazilian Amphibious Recon Sergeant – 1967.

This NCO is part of the Amphibious Reconnaissance Company of the Brazilian Marines. The members of this company who are all qualified as both paratroopers and frogmen have a mission similar to the U.S. Navy's SEALs and the USMC Recons. The sergeant illustrated wears the dress blue uniform of the Marines. A white uniform and a gray work uniform are also issued. His collar insignia and belt buckle both bear crossed rifles over anchor insignia. On his right breast is his parachutist's badge. Some amphibious recons also wear U.S. UDT or SEAL badges and/or U.S. parachutist's wings on their left breast since they have attended U.S. special schools. Colombian Lancero badges and, in a few cases, Portuguese jump badges, etc. will also be seen in wear by Brazilian Recons. His rank, third sergeant, is indicated by three chevrons under an anchor. A first sergeant wears five chevrons, a second sergeant four chevrons, and a corporal two chevrons, all with the anchor device.

93. Non-Aligned/Kenya: Kenyan Paratroop Corporal – 1967.

This paratrooper is part of Kenya's original paratroop company which received its jump training in Britain. He wears British pattern parachutist's (Denison) smock over olive green tropical trousers bloused into black combat boots. All in all, his uniform is very similar to that of the Parachute Regiment at the time. Instead of a red beret, however, he wears a green one. His webbed gear is also British 1944 pattern. Although he would have been awarded British parachutist's wings he wears Kenyan wings on his sleeve near the shoulder. Below the jump wings are his corporal's chevrons which are still in the style of the King's African Rifles of which he may be a veteran. His weapon is the Sterling Mk4 (L2A3) 9 mm. SMG with stock folded and 34 round magazine in place. Note that the magazine housing is on the side of the weapon rather than the bottom. Cyclic rate for the Sterling is 550 rpm.

94. Non-Aligned/Zaire: Zairean Paratroop Major – 1978.

This officer is very sharp looking in tailored French style 'cammies', highly polished jump boots, and red beret. On his right breast he wears his jump wings, while on his right hip he carries a Smith & Wesson .38 Special revolver. Whether the sun glasses are to protect his eyes from the African sun or to shield the thoughts contained in them from others involved in the deadly game of African power politics is open to question. Since the para/ commando forces in many African countries also function as bodyguards for the head of state, it is possible this major's sun shades serve the quite practical purpose of keeping potential assassins from knowing where he is looking. In any case, he looks to be a rather competent officer.

95. Non-Aligned/Congo: Congolese Para-Commando – 1978.

Although Congolese paras will be seen wearing a hodge podge of uniforms ranging from Italian and French camouflage to the spotted pattern illustrated, the light brown beret seems to be relatively standard. The parachutist's badge is worn on the left breast, with bars of rank below it on the pocket. His weapon is an AKM assault rifle, no doubt reflecting the Soviet/Cuban influence in the Congo.

96. Non-Aligned/Senegal: Senegalese Paratrooper – 1972.

This paratrooper is from one of Senegal's parachute companies. A French parachute company was still stationed in Senegal until 1974, and the French paras had a great influence on their African counterparts as this figure's camouflage illustrates.

22nd SAS, Coronation Park, Kuala Lumpur, Malaya. A simulated tree jumping exercise (*c.* 1957).

British paratroop major in full jumping gear. He wears the old style Denison smock.

Australian SAS troopers demonstrate their climbing skills in northern Australia.

Vietnam. Two U.S. Special Forces officers with local irregulars. The weapon is the M-79 Grenade Launcher.

Sergeant of the 1st Force Reconnaissance Company, 1st Marine Division, Camp Pendleton, 1974.

U.S. 82nd Airborne Military Police discuss their recent drop from Starlifters with the editor of *Reader's Digest*. (West Germany, Autumn, 1981).

French paratroop trainee at the French Army Parachute School at Pau.

Israeli para girls, ready to jump with their male comrades.